SOUTH SUDANESE PAST NOTES & RECORDS

Douglas H. Johnson

Africa World Books Pty Ltd.
P.O. Box 130 Wanneroo
WA 6065, Australia

ISBN 978-0-9943631-2-1

© *Douglas H. Johnson, 2015*
Foreword © *Taban lo Liyong, 2015*

All Rights Reserved. Except as permitted under current legislation no part of this work may be photocopied, stored in a retrieval system, published, performed in public, adapted, broadcast, transmitted, recorded or reproduced in any form or by any means without the prior permission of the copyright owner.

Dedicated to
South Sudanese historians,
past, present, and future

CONTENTS

Foreword by Prof. Taban lo Liyong   vii
Preface   xv

SELF-DETERMINATION AND INDEPENDENCE
1. Just what was the "Southern Policy"?   3
2. What was decided at the 1947 Juba Conference?   8
3. How many parties agreed to the 1952 "All Parties Agreement"?   13
4. The forgotten conference: Juba, 1954   18
5. The Torit Mutiny and the end of the British Empire   22
6. When South Sudanese became refugees   27
7. Just how did Sudan gain its independence?   32
8. How long did Sudan's first civil war last?   37
9. The trial of *The Vigilant* and press freedom in Sudan   42
10. 55 years of bananas   47
11. Sudan and the commonwealth   52
12. Friends and neighbours   56

PEOPLE
13. Languages of South Sudan   63
14. Are South Sudanese animists?   68
15. What did Ngundeng really say and do?   72
16. Is this Ngundeng's photograph?   77
17. South Sudanese Missionaries: Caterina Zeinab, translator and evangelist   81
18. South Sudanese Missionaries: Fr. Daniel Surur Farim Deng, slave and theologian   85
19. South Sudanese Missionaries: Salim Wilson, the "Black Evangelist of the North"   89
20. South Sudanese Soldiers: 'Ali Jaifun, a Shilluk soldier   95
21. South Sudanese Soldiers: Who won the Battle of Omdurman?   100
22. South Sudanese Soldiers: 'Ali 'Abd al-Latif and the White Flag League   107
23. South Sudanese Abroad: Nubis   113
24. South Sudan's Early Leaders: Stanislaus Paysama, slave and minister   118
25. South Sudan's Early Leaders: Logalis   123

PLACES
26 Whose names are on South Sudan's map? — 131
27 Rumbek and the zaribas of South Sudan — 136
28 Past states 1: "Greater" Upper Nile — 141
29 Past states 2: "Greater" Bahr el-Ghazal — 146
30 Past states 3: "Greater" Equatoria — 151
31 What was the purpose of the Jonglei Canal? — 156
32 What was the Wheatley-Munro agreement? — 161
33 How part of Western Bahr el-Ghazal became part of Southern Darfur — 166
34 How Chali and Yabus left the South — 171

LEGACIES
35 Why do we need Archives? — 179
36 How records were kept in South Sudan — 184
37 Is there a role for the amateur historian in South Sudan? — 189

SELECTED READING — 193

FIGURES

Figure 1	Map of South Sudan	iv
Figure 2	A Nuer Prophet	77
Figure 3	Salim Wilson	89
Figure 4	Officers of the 12th Sudanese Battalion	98
Figure 5	Sudanese Soldiers at Omdurman	102
Figure 6	The attack of the Black Flag	103
Figure 7	Macdonald's Manoeuvre	105
Figure 8	Banner of the New Sudan	111

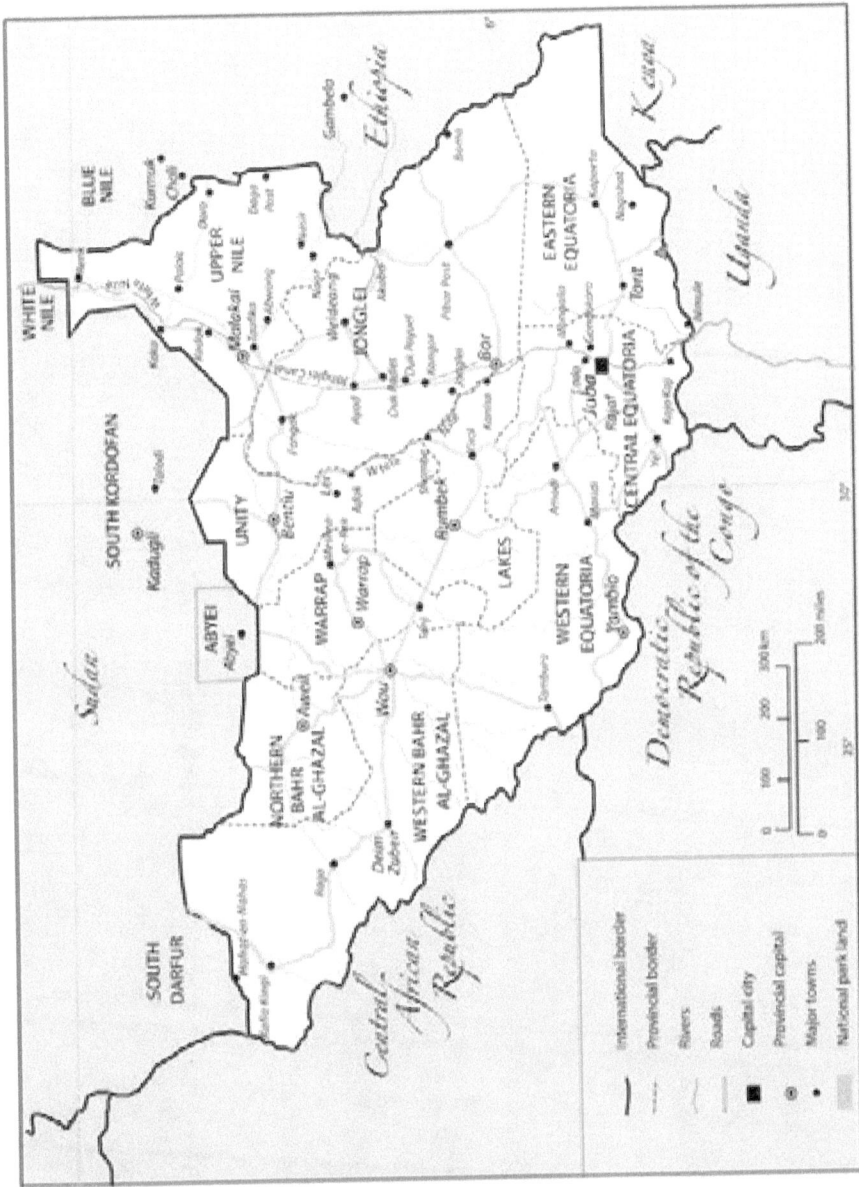

Figure 1: Map of South Sudan showing places mentioned in the text
(Kate Kirkwood, Kirkwood Publishing)

FOREWORD

Dr Douglas H. Johnson, the author of *South Sudanese Past Notes and Records* has asked me to write the foreword to his book. I have accepted the honour and am proceeding with the task of composing the foreword. Though he has already written a preface, which is satisfactory in itself, perhaps with an eye to the South Sudanese constituents whose story towards Independence these short documents retell, he must have thought a word from one of the sons of the soil would give them more legitimacy and acceptance.

I do not think he should have had some fear in that regard as the pieces speak for themselves and, as far as identification with our journey to nationhood, and standing by us in all the other difficult twists and turns of events after CPA are concerned, he has continued to guide us in this our/his adopted country.

I have used the word "guide" advisedly. Many an African nationalist baulks at using terms of endearment and praise to describe a European or American, both lumped as colonisers, imperialists, capitalists, and so forth. But in the writing of history, *our* history, have we got native sons and daughters who have become authoritative? The answer is resounding No! In the collection of archival materials that had been so painstakingly collected together, chiefly by Douglas? No. So, this small book is a guide to the foreigner who deserves the citizenship of South Sudan, real or honourary

A "foreword" by its very nature, consists of the introductory remarks, especially by a person other than the author. The author has already covered the field as much as he has delimited it. The forwarder's task is then to give an overview of the book drawing attention to its main thrusts, the gist of the matter, and in what way the book helps the seeker of knowledge or to deepen his or her knowledge, of the matters under review.

When the treasurer of the Candace (Queen of Ethiopia) was returning from Jerusalem to Ethiopia after the first Pentecost, St Philip the Apostle rode in his chariot and found him reading the book of Isaiah in which the event of the life and death of Jesus Christ were prophesied. St Philip asked him; "Do you understand what you are reading?" To that he answered truthfully; "How can I understand them unless another interpreted them to me?" whereupon St Philip proceeded to tell him that it was this same Jesus whose death anniversary he, the treasurer, had participated in honouring whose life story was prophesied.

I find most of us South Sudanese in the same boat as that treasurer. Reading documents about our past but not being able to understand them properly because we lack the proper background and international context into which to situate them. We had the English, the "Anglo" component of the Anglo-Egyptian Sudanese Condominium. Being part of one of the oldest colonial European nations in modern history and the one who came out winner in amassing colonies in the Americas, Asia and Africa, most certainly the British were no children playing with us. For them, the Suez Canal, a sea-path to their crown jewel possessions of India, Malaya (today Malaysia), Australia and New Zealand, leave alone Fiji and other smaller islands, events in the Sudan were discussed in the wider context of British colonies abroad that brought in raw materials and were markets for "home" products. So, an event such as the "Southern policy" that launched discussion about us, and that produced a policy to deal with us, was made in the wider context of outwitting Egypt and keeping the sea-route flowing with goods. That is also where the 1947 Juba Conference fitted. Northern Sudanese politicians wanted instant independence. Did they know how primitive Southern Sudanese were? So opined the British. What was the purpose of keeping us in "closed districts" if not to keep us backward? In any future desires of Northern Sudanese demanding independence (hot water), then pour (very cold water) on South Sudanese, so that there would be an explosion. Egypt wanted unity with the Sudan. Oh yes? Well embroil the Sudan in a civil war (started in 1955) and see if Egypt would still want that unity. Meanwhile the Suez Canal lets the ships go to the East and back to England. Though it is little known or suspected, the Torit mutineers report that they were encouraged to rebel by the British junior officers who said this was the Southerners' only chance to remain under British protection once Northern Sudan had got independence and their cherished unity with Egypt. Their rude awakening was when Britain sent 8,000 troops to crush the mutiny.[1]

Egypt too had its designs. Why did it want unity with the Sudan? In order to ensure the flow of the Nile waters. And let it be a united Sudan because you never can tell what the South Sudanese would do, leave alone the Ugandans and the other East African States. That is also why the Jonglei Canal was planned, originally with the help of British engineers and later excavated by French engineers. The reasons for the canal are given us in the chapter: "What was the purpose of the Jonglei Canal?"

Since most people do not pay serious attention to their readings of documents concerning our past, Douglas gives us a detailed reading (or rereading) of "What was decided at the 1947 Juba Conference?" including who made the most crucial decision: the civil secretary, J. Robertson. If on the first day of the meeting Southerners, mostly chiefs, had held out against going to Khartoum to participate in the party politics, but the junior administrative officers, led by Clement Mboro – cared more about "equal pay for equal qualifications and equal grades" with the Northerners, the North had an astute wheeler-dealer – Mohammed Effendi Shingeiti, possibly of Moroccan descent, who knew exactly what the Northerners wanted done: to

---

[1] My pet theory is: what did the British junior officers or simply officers, tell the soldiers in Torit leading to their mutiny? My information comes from mutineers who slept in my father's home on their way to Kampala, in Bobi, 16 miles south of Gulu, in 1955.

bulldoze Southerners to go and participate in parliamentary debate in order to bring the date for self determination closer. According to Stanislaus Paysama's autobiography, after the first day's meetings Shingeiti met him when he was already despairing about Southern representation. Shingeiti berated him and his primitive chiefs. At night, after filing the chief's with *'aragi*, they were so drowsy the following day, that they had a change of mind. They were going to Khartoum to participate in the political discussions. After all, their sons Stanislaus and Clement, who were the equals of Northerners in education, had assured them that some Northern tribes were more primitive than they, and yet they were going to the parliament.

The civil secretary confessed to Prince Walter Kunijwok, that he decided on his own to bind the fate of Southern Sudan into that of the Sudan after drinking nine cups of stiff coffee. (In the place of "nine cups of stiff coffee" please read nine double tots of neat whisky/Johnny Walker).

According to Douglas, reading of the general picture, the Juba 1954 Conference planned and executed by Southern intellectuals and intelligentsia deserves a lot of study and scrutiny, even though South Sudanese political activists afterwards never referred to it in subsequent discussions.

How did Sudan get its independence? Or how quickly, did affairs move so that (a) the Mahdists who had wanted national independence had their role taken over by the National Unionist Party who had advocated Unity with Egypt? So that South Sudanese divided and forgot about the 1954 resolutions? So that even the British governor-general was no longer there at the lowering of the Union Jack and the hoisting of the National flag on January 1,1956 making the Sudan the first colony in Africa, South of the Sahara to get independence, followed by Ghana in 1957?

There are some unfinished businesses all the same. Douglas is not sure if we know what the Nuer Lou prophet Ngundeng said and did. Nor whether the composite photo of a dead prophet's looking man with a pipe is that of Ngundeng.

Who has greater claims to Ali Abd al-Latif? His Northern father's people, or us, his mother's people, or the Sudan's general independence politics?

The battle of Omdurman, Douglas seems to suggest was won mainly by contingents of Southern soldiers.

He also unearthed the little-known document that described the Wheatley-Munro agreement about boundaries between Bahr el Ghazal and Southern Kordofan. As well as an explanation of how part of Bahr el Ghazal became part of southern Darfur.

In the manner of: look, you have let part of your land to go. Are you sure you want Chali and Yabus too to leave the South forever? He made us aware of our laws without a fight over parts of our patrimony. (There are other lost areas to our east, south, and west).

When we see our history has played havoc with our life, Douglas wishes we had native historians of our own as national archivists. History is written by the victors, nationalistically. Decolonisers show how the nation was born and passed this information to the born and those to be born as part of their heritage. That is why we need historians of South Sudan.

So, starting with little known facts about generally well-known events in our recent past, Douglas also tells about South Sudanese abroad, who started off their missions optimistically perhaps with more enthusiasm in them than circumspection, only to suffer rude awakening when they found themselves abused or misused. It is as if the tamed leopard would never leave its spots nor desire for blood and flesh all the South

Sudanese abroad whose stories he tells ended up disillusioned by the company they kept especially northerners, Italians, Egyptians and other Europeans, and the colleagues they worked with, or who were their employers.

Had we known what had happened to our people abroad over 100 years ago, perhaps we would not have trusted British junior officers in Torit who had told us to rebel in expectation of salvation from the Egyptians and Northern Sudanese. For why did the Torit soldiers believe the British junior officers, if not blind trust, or plain ignorance of international affairs? When Northern politicians told our junior politicians to jump headlong into independence because our cherished "federalism would be given consideration", was that a guarantee that would have stood serious scrutiny in a court of law to mean "South Sudanese were promised federation"? Did Northern politicians under their first speaker – no other than Shingieti of the 1947 Juba Conference – not "give federalism serious consideration" and found it, as they say, unsuited for the Sudan?

About this word-game and others Sayed Abel Alier was to title his book *Too Many Agreements Dishonoured*. But perhaps they were made in jest, or were they simple word play by masters of the word? With geniuses in language use like lawyers Shengeiti and Hassan al-Turabi one had better use advanced English dictionary and its Arabic equivalent (is it Elias?) to decipher the meanings, innuendos, *double entendres*, allusions from Arabic lore, French sophistication and English compendia in order to assure oneself that one had really fathomed their meanings.

A beginning in making us sophisticates has begun with this book. I hope we read these pieces with fine combs. If possible read them and then revisit the documents they are referring too, for Christians are urged to learn to read so that they can read the word by themselves. So, let us reread the various documents commented on here to check if we had understood them right.

The legacies of Douglas H. Johnson are these: we need archives and particularly archivists. The record keeping we inherited from the past needs re-ordering. And finally, if it will take long to get professional historians, we should, at least have amateur historians for our Bomas and Payams, to begin with. Having called and proved Douglas a guide, and pointed out how that title fits him, I am sure my part as the provider of a foreword is finished. If the elaborations I have provided have stimulated the reader to find out what Douglas wrote, and learned about some ancient matters concerning us then I feel honoured. But I am not as timid as Douglas to urge for the birth of amateur historians. We look forward to the rise of fully pledged professional historians of South Sudan.

Period!

Taban lo Liyong
University of Juba
Staff Club
August 16, 2012

PREFACE

This collection of articles first appeared in the *The Pioneer* weekly newspaper. Its founding editor, Atem Yaak Atem, invited me to contribute a weekly column of historical pieces that we decided to entitle "Past Notes and Records". Back in the early 1980s when we were colleagues in the Regional Ministry of Culture and Information I had written a series of articles called "The Streets of Juba" for *Southern Sudan Magazine*, which Atem had also founded. In those articles I gave brief biographies of some of the famous South Sudanese after whom some of Juba's main streets had been named, and in many ways "Past Notes and Records" is a continuation and expansion of that earlier series.

The pieces are intended to inform and to stimulate discussion and debate. The history of South Sudan has been a neglected subject. Much of the academic history about South Sudan has been written about foreign rulers rather than about South Sudanese communities and individuals. The history of South Sudan and South Sudanese was not included in the Sudan school syllabuses and is usually excluded from the general political histories of Sudan. There is still no reliable textbook on South Sudanese history for use in its schools. South Sudanese may know something about the past of their own communities, but few have had the opportunity to learn much about the broad history of their nation or how it fits into the wider region.

The columns in this collection were originally addressed to a South Sudanese readership, and it is primarily for that readership, both at home and abroad, that they are republished here. This book is neither a comprehensive overview of South Sudan's past, nor a record of the most important events or historic personalities. It is more like a selection of snapshots from a family album. The re-discovery of the past and the writing of history is a never-ending process. This booklet is only a beginning, a small offering to mark South Sudan's achievement of independence. It is an open invitation to South Sudanese to research and write more about their own past.

I wish to acknowledge Kate Kirkwood of Kirkwood Publishing for the map of South Sudan that accompanies this volume, and the Pitt Rivers Museum, Oxford and the University of Durham for permission to reprint the photographs that appear as figures 2 and 4.

Douglas H. Johnson
Oxford, 2015

SELF-DETERMINATION AND INDEPENDENCE

1
JUST WHAT WAS THE "SOUTHERN POLICY"?

The "Southern Policy" of the Anglo-Egyptian government in Sudan has been blamed for many things. Politicians, journalists, and ordinary citizens often claim that it meant that the South was administered separately from the North, that it excluded all Arabs and Muslims and actively eliminated all Arab and Muslim influences from the South, that it created a tribal "zoo" in the South, that it kept the South under-developed. But just what was the "Southern Policy", how long did it last, and what was its effect?

The "re-conquest" of Sudan was undertaken by Britain to re-establish Egypt's control over its former colony. The army that overthrew the Mahdist state at Omdurman in 1898 was largely an Egyptian army with Egyptian and Sudanese troops and British officers. It was the army that provided the administrative structure and personnel that governed the country, with British officers as provincial governors and inspectors, and Egyptian and Sudanese officers as mamurs and sub-mamurs, the local government officials of the day.

In the North pacification was completed relatively quickly and there was an early transition from military to civil administration, with more civilians – British and Sudanese – appointed to administrative posts. But in the South pacification took longer. By and large South Sudanese peoples did not see the advancing Anglo-Egyptian force as liberators, because they had already liberated themselves from the Mahdist theocracy. There was a far longer period of resistance to the Anglo-Egyptian government in the South than in the North — in fact, the last pacification campaign in the whole of British Africa was fought against the Nuer in 1927-30. One result of this was that administration in the South continued to be dominated by military personnel and military interests up into the 1920s. While in the North Sudanese were being trained at Gordon

Memorial College (later the University of Khartoum) for posts in the expanding civil administration, in the South the government decided that it needed only a few "moderately educated Blacks" to fill minor clerical posts and there was very little investment in education.

Two things changed in the 1920s: the introduction of "Native Administration" and the expulsion of the Egyptian army. Native Administration, or Indirect Rule, was founded on the principle of administering rural areas through customary authorities, using customary law. This applied to both northern and southern provinces, and while sharia or Islamic law was also applied as family law in the North, local customs within different Muslim communities were also recognised. In the South sharia law applied only in those towns with significant Muslim populations, and customary law, applied through the chiefs' courts, became the basis for local administration. Already with the introduction of Native Administration in 1921 the role of the mamur was becoming superfluous, but the expulsion of Egyptian soldiers following the White Flag Mutiny in Khartoum in 1924, and the formation of a separate Sudan Defence Force, independent of Egypt, meant that by 1925 the mamur had virtually (but not completely) disappeared from the rural areas. Those who remained were almost exclusively northern Sudanese civilians; very few Southerners were recruited into junior administrative posts outside of the main towns until much later.

Native Administration, then, was the policy for the entire country. It meant that rural administration was based increasingly on customary law and vernacular languages. It was one system, but it allowed for and encouraged the development of local variations. In the South this meant encouraging development along local custom, which, for the most part, was not influenced by Islam. This new system of Native Administration in the South was further reinforced by the Closed Districts Ordinance, first introduced in 1922.

Throughout the British Empire colonial governments imposed closed district regulations on areas allegedly in need of protection from illegal or damaging economic (and sometimes political) activity. In parts of East Africa some frontier districts were declared closed in order to combat poaching. In the Sudan districts were declared closed usually as a means of combating the surreptitious slave-trade that was still being conducted even in the 1920s, and which Egypt and Britain, as members of the League of Nations, were committed to eradicating. Most parts of the South (Renk District excluded), and some parts of Blue Nile, the Nuba Mountains and Darfur were declared Closed Districts and persons from outside those districts (merchants, hunters, tourists) had to apply for permits to enter. Movements between districts by local peoples continued to be regulated through the institutions of Native Administration.

In 1930 these different strands of administrative practice were brought together in a policy memorandum issued by the civil secretary (head of civil government) in Khartoum "to build up a series of self-contained racial and tribal units with structure and organization based, to whatever extent the requirements of equity and good government permit, upon indigenous customs, traditional usage and beliefs." In practical terms this meant the continued reduction of the role of the mamur, the use of vernacular languages in rural administration, the development of customary law through a network of chiefs' courts, and the recognition and definition of specific tribal territories. It also meant that non-Arab merchants (Greeks, Armenians and Christian Lebanese) were given priority in permits to trade.

The newly articulated Southern Policy was interpreted in different ways in different provinces. In Bahr el-Ghazal British officials went to extremes in the Western District in creating a No-Man's Land with Darfur around Kafia Kingi, of expelling certain Darfur peoples, and even of eliminating Arabic personal names (see chapter 33). This exaggerated and heavy-handed application of the policy went beyond what the civil secretary had intended, and many British administrators in other parts of the South were shocked and appalled. The example of the Western District of Bahr el-Ghazal has since been cited as typical of the Southern Policy, but in fact it was unique.

The Southern Policy lasted for only sixteen years. It was abandoned in 1946 when the government adopted the policy of self-government and self-determination for the whole of the Sudan in order to prevent Egypt from asserting its sovereignty over its own colony. But what was the overall impact of those sixteen years?

Did the Southern Policy mean that the South was administered "separately" from the North? No. The southern provinces were part of the same administrative system as the whole of Sudan, sharing the same administrative personnel, and subject to the same administrative regulations. The Southern Policy was seen as a logical extension of the principles of Native Administration, based on local custom, and the local customs of most of the southern peoples were markedly different from the local customs of most Muslim peoples in the northern provinces. The policy allowed for, and encouraged, a wider diversity of customs.

Did the Southern Policy exclude all Muslims from the South? No. There were a number of indigenous Muslim communities in the main towns, notably Renk, Kodok, Malakal, Wau, Rumbek and Juba who were unaffected by this policy. And while Northern Sudanese petty traders were usually denied permits to trade, local Muslim Southern Sudanese traders often acted as agents of larger Northern firms.

Were northern Sudanese completely prevented from entering the South? No. Pastoralist peoples such as the Rizeigat, Misseriya, Seleim and Rufa'a continued to cross the border in their seasonal migrations and continued to mingle with southern border peoples. Northern Sudanese employed in a number of technical departments, such as the Railways and Steamers, served in the South. Not all mamurs were removed. Two of the Khalifa Abdallahi's sons served as mamurs in Upper Nile. Ibrahim Bedri, related to the family that founded what became Ahlia University in Omdurman, served as a mamur in Yirol and Renk, spoke Dinka, and trained southern administrators such as Clement Mboro. Merchants from major trading houses in the Three Towns also continued to trade in the South throughout the period of the Southern Policy.

Did the Southern Policy keep Northerners and Southerners separate? Only to a certain extent. The Southern Policy did nothing to build up a unified corps of Sudanese administrators, trained in the same institutions and serving together throughout the country. The government's decision to limit the number of Southerners in the civil service was taken in the early years of the twentieth century, and the Southern Policy did little to reverse this.

Did the Southern Policy keep the South undeveloped? The Southern Policy was a symptom of the government's economic neglect of most of the rural areas of Sudan, not its cause. Other rural areas of the North remained undeveloped under Native Administration.

The Southern Policy, therefore, was a brief episode in the history of British administration of the Sudan. It may have helped to emphasize the differences between the peoples of the South and the peoples of the North, but it did not create them. It cannot take all the blame for the civil wars that followed independence.

Further reading:
    Robert O. Collins, *Shadows in the Grass: Britain in the Southern Sudan, 1918-1956*
    Lilian Passmore Sanderson & Neville Sanderson, *Education, Religion & Politics in Southern Sudan 1899-1964*

2
WHAT WAS DECIDED AT THE 1947 JUBA CONFERENCE?

The Juba Conference of 12-13 June 1947 has often been cited as the event in which South Sudanese chose to become part of a united Sudan. But what was the Juba Conference, who attended it, and just what was decided? To answer these questions we must first understand the political context of the time.

Sudan's colonial status was unique in twentieth century Africa: in effect it was a colony of a colony. In international law it belonged to Egypt, but Egypt was under British occupation and control, and Britain administered Sudan through an article of the Anglo-Egyptian Treaty. After the end of World War Two Egypt insisted on re-negotiating the treaty and tried to re-assert its sovereignty over Sudan. Britain countered by supporting not only Sudanese self-government, but self-determination (a principle it was not offering its own colonies at the time). Moves were made to convert the Advisory Council of the northern Sudan into a Legislative Assembly. The question then arose, would self-government and self-determination be for the North only, or for the entire country?

British administrative policy in Sudan had, since 1930, kept open the possibility that the southern provinces might one day be transferred to colonial authority in British East Africa. This was an option that remained theoretical but was not actively pursued: it could not be done as long as Egypt refused. With Egypt now attempting to reassert its sovereignty over its own colony, and with northern nationalists demanding self-determination within Sudan's geographical boundaries, a separate administrative future for the southern Sudan was no longer even a theoretical possibility, and the Sudan government prepared a new policy linking the South's future inextricably with that of the North. But some consultation with the educated leadership of the South – junior administrative officials, policemen, teachers, and chiefs – was deemed necessary, if only for form's sake, and early in 1947, following the recommendation of the Sudan Administration Conference that southern representatives be included in the new Legislative Assembly, the civil secretary, J.W. Robertson, circulated heads of departments and southern provincial governors a memo outlining the change in policy and instructing them to take soundings of southern educated opinion.

The results of this consultation are preserved in Robertson's papers in the Sudan Archive at the University of Durham, UK, and a few responses of southern Sudanese civil servants, along with the minutes of the Juba Conference, have been published in Yosa Wawa's book, *Southern Sudanese Pursuits of Self-Determination: documents in political history*. They were asked: 1) should the South remain with the North, be joined to Uganda, or be entirely separate, 2) should the South be subject to a Legislative Assembly composed of northern Sudanese only, 3) should southern Sudanese be appointed to that Legislative Assembly, or 4) should the affairs of the South be governed by a separate parliament in the South?

The majority of the opinions forwarded to Robertson were nearly unanimous in rejecting incorporation into Uganda; only four repudiated amalgamation with the North; all rejected the idea of the southern provinces being governed by a northern parliament without southern representation; some wanted southern representatives in Khartoum, while others wanted a separate southern parliament. In presenting their answers many cited a distrust of Northerners based on historical experience within living memory, others cited religious differences, but many also made comparisons with contemporary events elsewhere in the world.

These responses enabled Robertson to plan for the Juba Conference, where only three of the respondents (Siricio Iro, Hassan Fertak and Clement Mboro) were chosen to attend. All three had written against the option of a separate South. Those most critical of unity with the North were not invited. Additional junior officials (such as Buth Diu) and a selection of chiefs (including James Tembura, Lolik Lado, and chief Lapponya) were also appointed.

The other participants in the conference included the British governors of Upper Nile, Equatoria and the deputy governor of Bahr el-Ghazal sub-province. Northern delegates included Ibrahim Bedri, Dr Habib Abdalla, and Judge Muhammed Saleh Shingeiti. Both Ibrahim Bedri and Dr Habib had worked in the South: Ibrahim Bedri even spoke Dinka. Shingeiti had also been a junior administrator before joining the judiciary. An active member of the Ummah Party, his racial attitudes were perhaps typical of the time. As sub-mamur in Jebelein in the 1920s he once described the Shilluk as "one of the laziest tribes of the Negroes", and exclaimed that "the wonderful thing" about the Seleim Baggara was that despite intermarriage with Shilluk and Dinka, they "have been able to preserve their own tongue and their good features. They are a good looking race..."

In gauging the performance of the southern delegates, one must remember the hierarchy of the Sudan government. Robertson was the head of the civil administration. He was one step below the governor-general, and the governors were one step below him, each nearly supreme in his own province. The southern representatives all came from the lowest levels of that administration: the highest ranks present were a sub-mamur and a Police sergeant-major. It was as if a field marshall and his staff had descended on a sergeants' mess, urging them to speak their minds freely. A few did, but most were reticent.

The terms of reference circulated to the delegates dealt with southern representation in the proposed Legislative Assembly and the possibility of an Advisory Council for the southern Sudan. But with the responses to his questionnaire in mind Robertson felt confident to reduce the agenda to one basic question: "whether they considered that the South was essentially to be one with the North". When discussions following from that question began to revolve around whether the South should have its own advisory council, he again brought the conference around to the question of the unity of Sudan:

> The Chairman asked whether anybody present had any objections to the Unity of Sudan.
> Mohd. Saleh Eff. Shingeiti complained that this was outside the meeting's terms of reference but the Civil Secretary refused to admit this. The Civil Secretary again addressed the meeting and said that if nobody spoke on this subject, then they would assume agreement on the principle of the Unity of the Sudan.
> Chief Lapponya stated that the principle of unity could only be decided later when the Southerners were grown up, by which time they would be in a position to decide whether to join the North or go to the Belgian Congo or Uganda.
> The Chairman explained that people could not get up and go where they like just like that.

Seeing the direction Robertson was steering the meeting, Shingeiti became the most vocal advocate for national unity. Summing up the discussion Robertson concluded "that most Southerners present (Shingeiti Eff. 'All of them.') were agreed that the Sudan was one country," though in fact only three of the sixteen southern delegates had spoken on the subject, and only one of them had accepted (with some reservations) the idea that Sudan was one country. Thus this first group of southern leaders to be brought into consultation about the future of Sudan found that the option of southern self-determination was not even to be discussed, and that they were required, by their silence, to acquiesce in a unity that had already been decided for them.

Robertson admitted on the second day of the conference that it was only exploratory and could take no decisions by itself. Following a night of some lobbying by Shingeiti and Dr Habib, and long discussions late in the night with Stanislaus Paysama – then a clerk in the civil secretary's office in Khartoum – the southern delegates were persuaded that Southerners should participate as appointed members in the new Legislative Assembly in Khartoum (see chapter 24). This was the agreement Robertson wanted, but it was an administrative arrangement only, not a constitutional decision, and was reported as such to the British Foreign Office. As Robertson wrote many years later, "I looked upon the conference solely as a means of finding out the capabilities of the Southerners, and it was therefore quite inaccurate for some people to say later that at the Juba conference the southern representatives agreed to come in with the North. No decisions could be made at the conference, since members had received no mandate from their peoples ... The only decision resulting from the conference was taken by myself". As he admitted many years later to Dr. Walter Kunijwok, he made this decision after drinking nine cups of coffee. This raises the question, would the future of the South have been different had Robertson been drinking tea?

The Juba conference was the first time that the collective opinion of southern Sudanese was formally canvassed. As such the event has taken on a greater significance than it was given at the time. It was one step on the way towards the administrative and legislative integration of the South with the North, but it left the issue of southern self-determination unresolved. That would be left to another Juba conference.

Further reading:
    J.W. Robertson, *Transition in Africa: from direct rule to independence*
    Dunstan M. Wai, *The African-Arab Conflict in the Sudan*
    Yosa Wawa, *Southern Sudanese Pursuits of Self-Determination: documents in political history*

3
HOW MANY PARTIES AGREED TO THE 1952 "ALL PARTIES AGREEMENT"?

The All Parties Agreement of 11 January 1953 between Egypt and the main northern Sudanese parties of the day has often been cited as the first betrayal of the southern Sudan by the North. The agreement set out the terms for the transition of Sudan to self-government and self-determination. This was the first time that an Egyptian government recognized the Sudanese right to self-determination, but the agreement also weakened the (British) governor-general's discretionary powers in relation to the three southern provinces, and as a blue-print for the self-government period it had been drawn up without consulting a single southern Sudanese leader. So just who were the parties to this agreement, what were the implications of the agreement, and why was it considered a betrayal of the South?

Sudan was a colony of Egypt administered by Britain according to the terms of the Anglo-Egyptian Treaty of 1936, which also covered Britain's occupation of the Suez Canal and its military bases in Egypt. The treaty came up for re-negotiation in 1946, and surprisingly the most contentious issue was not Britain's military presence in Egypt, but the future of Sudan. The Egyptian government insisted on a formal recognition of the sovereignty of the Egyptian monarch over Sudan. Britain countered this by recognizing Sudan's right not only to self-government, but to self-determination, and even promising the possibility of full independence in twenty years. With negotiations over the treaty deadlocked, Britain began preparing the way for Sudanese self-government. This involved the creation of a Legislative Assembly in Khartoum, the convening of the Juba Conference in 1947 to find out if there were southern Sudanese willing to become part of the Assembly (chapter 2), and the re-organization of local government away from the Native Administration of the past, and towards new, more bureaucratic, town and province councils.

Among the Sudanese, however, there was disagreement about how self-determination would be achieved and what, exactly, it would determine. The most vocal party in support of complete independence was the Ummah party, backed by the Ansar sect then led by the Mahdi's son, Sayyid Abd al-Rahman al-Mahdi, grandfather of Sadiq al-Mahdi. But there were other northern Sudanese, particularly the Khatmiyya sect of the Mirghani family, who feared a return of a Mahdiya under Sayyid Abd al-Rahman (or SAR as he was known), and therefore were opposed to the Ummah party's vision of independence under their rule.

The Khatmiyya sect had close ties to Egypt, while the British administration of Sudan encouraged the Ummah's anti-Egyptian stance. Thus northern Sudan's internal politics – pro-Ansar vs. anti-Ansar – intersected with Sudan's international politics – pro-independence vs. pro-unity with Egypt. Many of those suspicious of SAR's intentions (it was widely feared the British would make him king of the Sudan, as they had done with the Hashemite kings in Jordan and Iraq, and were to do with Idris in Libya) sided with the pro-Egyptian Ashigga party. A compromise between the two was attempted with the formation of the pro-independence, non-Ansar, Socialist Republican Party in 1951, led by Ibrahim Bedri, a former administrator in the South. The SRP hoped to gain support among pro-independence Khatmiyya, non-Mahdist rural constituencies, and Southerners. By 1951 there were thus a number of parties in the North, both pro-independence and pro-union with Egypt, but none yet in the South.

In 1948 a national Legislative Assembly was created to prepare the country for self-government. The pro-unionist parties claimed that it was a tool of the British and boycotted it. The South was represented by only 14% of the Assembly's seats, the rest going to the Ummah and rural, or "country" constituencies. The pro-unionist parties did agree to serve on the thirteen-member Constitutional Amendment Commission, on which the South had a single vote. The Commission was supposed to draft the self-government statute that would become the country's interim constitution throughout the period leading to self-determination.

Southern representatives in the Assembly and on Commission pushed hard for a federal constitution with a separate Ministry of Southern Affairs headed by a southern minister, but this was voted down by the northern majority in 1952. A compromise of sorts was reached in the draft self-government bill, giving the British governor-general special discretionary powers regarding the South. It is important to remember that the compromise embodied in the final draft self-government statute had been agreed to by the unionist members of the Commission and the Ummah representatives in the Assembly. The statute had to be presented to the two co-dominal powers for approval before it was enacted, but events in Egypt delayed presentation.

In 1950 King Farouk, under political pressure at home, announced his intention of abrogating the Anglo-Egyptian Treaty, whose re-negotiation had stalled over the issue of Sudan. He put this threat into effect in October 1951, leaving the Sudan in something of a legal limbo: did the Condominium still exist, or not? But in July 1952 the Free Officers coup, led by Abd al-Gamal Nasser and Muhammad Neguib, overthrew Farouk and indicated a willingness to reach an agreement with Britain over Sudan. At the same time the Egyptians made direct approaches to the northern parties, even creating a new one for the purpose. At Egyptian insistence (and with its financial backing) the pro-unionist, anti-Ansar parties were merged to become the National Union Party (NUP), the predecessor to today's DUP. In October 1952 Neguib announced an agreement with the Ummah party, accepting self-government and providing for a transitional period in which the dual administration of the condominium would be liquidated to create a "free and neutral atmosphere" for self-determination. A new commission would be created above the governor-general, and many of his reserved powers were to be transferred to the commission. This was soon followed by parallel agreements with the SRP and NUP.

Who was responsible for weakening the governor-general's powers in relation to the South? At first it was assumed that the Egyptians had done so, as both the Ummah and unionist parties had agreed to this provision in the self-government statute. But it soon emerged that this was not the case. In discussions with the British Neguib was sympathetic to reinstating the governor-general's reserved powers, but he revealed that the more restrictive provisions had been insisted on by the NUP and the Ummah party – the Ummah in particular. This became clearer in January 1953 when at a meeting in Cairo Egypt concluded an All Parties Agreement with the Ummah, NUP, SRP and Watan (National) party. It was further reported that both the Ummah and NUP threatened to boycott elections to the new parliament if Britain insisted on retaining safeguards for the South. The All Parties Agreement thus became the basis on which a new self-government statute was agreed, and the basis on which elections for Sudan's first self-government prior to self-determination were held.

The Foreign Office in London suspected that northern Sudanese politicians were more eager than the Egyptians to remove the British from the South prior to self-determination. These suspicions were confirmed by SAR's own reaction. Britain reminded SAR that it was only because of the inclusion of guarantees in the draft self-government statute that southern members of the Legislative Assembly had agreed to co-operate in a unitary constitution for the country. He responded that he would not personally go against the agreement, "which the Southerners would have to accept in their best interests." He went on to warn, "Let the South boycott the elections if they wished: should they do so, Parliament would have to make an arrangement later."

This repudiation by the northern parties of a statute they had already accepted through debate and negotiation with southern parliamentarians stimulated the formation of organized political activity in the South. A Southern Sudan Political Emergency Committee was formed to organize protests against the agreement and wired the British foreign secretary, "It is very surprising to see that the Southern Sudan with a population, of about one third of the entire Sudan population, cannot take part in deciding the future of the country." It went on to add prophetically, "unless Northerners compromise with us, it will be very difficult to establish a government, which assures equality of treatment to all…" Shortly after this the South's first political party, the Liberal Party, was formed.

The politics of exclusion from negotiations of national importance eventually continued in reverse. In 2002-5 it was the northern parties – including the Ummah and DUP – who were excluded from the Machakos and Naivasha peace talks. What effect that will have on the lasting peace and stability of Sudan and South Sudan remains to be seen.

Further reading:
    Douglas H. Johnson (ed.), *Sudan, 1942-1950*
    Douglas H. Johnson (ed.), *Sudan, 1951-1956*
    Peter Woodward, *Condominium and Sudanese Nationalism*

4
THE FORGOTTEN CONFERENCE: JUBA, 1954

We all know about the 1947 Juba Conference (or at least we think we do). Its minutes have been reprinted in numerous collections, its importance and impact discussed, dissected and debated over at least forty-five years. But there was another, later Juba Conference, one far less well known, but possibly of greater lasting importance to the history – and future – of the Southern Sudan: the "Buth Diu" Conference of 1954, so named after its principle organizer. For it was at this conference that the southern leadership of the day announced the conditions on which they would accept a united Sudan, and reserved the South's right of self-determination.

Sudan was well on the path to independence by 1954. The Self-Government Act of 1953, agreed between Britain and Egypt, laid out the stages by which Sudan would first achieve self-government and then move on to self-determination. Nation-wide parliamentary elections would be held at the end of 1953, and on the basis of these elections the majority party would form a new government with an all-Sudanese cabinet, led by a Sudanese prime minister, with the governor-general taking the role of head of state advised by a governor-general's commission of Sudanese. Parliament would oversee the Sudanisation of the army, police, civil administration, and when Sudanisation was completed would petition the co-dominal powers to hold simultaneously a constitutional referendum and new parliamentary elections. The referendum would pose two options for the future of Sudan: unity with Egypt or complete independence. The new parliament would then convene as a Constituent Assembly to draft and pass a constitution reflecting the outcome of the referendum.

The pro-Egyptian National Union Party (NUP) won a majority of seats in the 1953 elections and formed the first government with Ismail al-Azhari as prime minister. The newly-formed

Liberal Party won many of the South's parliamentary seats, but a number of independent candidates were also elected. Many of these joined the NUP, and three were appointed ministers in the new government. The southern leadership thus became divided over the future direction of the nation and the South's place within it: unity with Egypt, or independence? And if independent, what form of government should that take? It was at this point that some southern leaders began to propose a federal constitution for the whole country.

In order to debate the issue further Buth Diu, a founding member of the Liberal Party, organized the first pan-southern conference (or South-South conference to use today's terminology) to meet in Juba in October 1954. It included some 250 delegates from all three southern provinces, including a number of chiefs from the rural areas, representatives from the southern Diaspora in Khartoum, and seven southern members of the ruling NUP (the three southern ministers were also invited but declined to respond). Its deliberations were conducted in English but translated into five other languages: Bari, Zande, Latuka, Dinka and Arabic. It debated two main questions: the political future of the Sudan as a whole, and the political future of the South, with the intention of Southerners arriving at a common position on these two issues prior to the elections that were to decide them. The only known set of minutes of the conference can now be found in the Foreign Office files in the National Archives in Kew, United Kingdom (the transcript has been published in Yosa Wawa's *Southern Sudanese Pursuits of Self-Determination: documents in political history*).

Benjamin Lwoki was elected to the chair of the conference and opened the first day of discussion by drawing the delegates' attention to the historic nature of the conference as "the first time in the History of the Sudan for the Three Southern Provinces" to come together "in the Struggle of the Sudan towards independence and Ultimate self Determination." An agenda was tabled for discussion of: the political future of the

Sudan as a whole, the political future of the South within a united Sudan, the NUP government's platform of unity with Egypt, and economic development and education in the South.

In the debate that followed speakers made a number of points that showed how closely southern Sudanese had been following the national political debate. The first speaker to raise the issue of separation was Chief Kuol Col of Bor, who argued that if the Sudan were to unite with Egypt, then the South should separate. Other speakers agreed. The question was then raised whether Sudan should be a republic or a monarchy – an indirect reference to the widespread fear that Sayyid Abd al-Rahman al-Mahdi hoped to become king of Sudan. The conference then voted on two motions: should the Sudan be independent or join with Egypt, and should Sudan have a president or a monarch. In both votes the conference voted 217 to 0 for independence and for a presidential system (the NUP members present abstained).

Having thus backed independence for the Sudan, the conference debated what kind of independence this would be. It was a Shilluk representative, Attillion Attor, who first proposed federation as the best system to guard against exploitation of the South within a united Sudan. It was left to Stanislaus Paysama, a senator from Bahr el-Ghazal, to give a detailed description of federal systems to the conference, an explanation that had to be translated into Arabic as well as the other languages of the South and took two and a quarter hours. The minutes record that "by then the house was well informed with meaning of Federation".

The subsequent debate showed strong support for the idea of federation, but with different applications. Buth Diu reminded the conference that federation did not mean separation, but was an alternative to it. Several speakers, including one Musa Beshir, part of the southern Diaspora in Khartoum, broadened the application of federation to include not just the South, but the Nuba, Fur and Funj: i.e. what are now Southern Kordofan,

Darfur and Blue Nile. This idea received considerable support. The motion in favour of a federal system was passed by a vote of 227 to 0, with the NUP delegates again abstaining. The minutes of the conference conclude, "From the above votes Southerners are out for *federation*. If this is not possible we request explanation otherwise the alternative can be taken and that is – 'separation.'"

The results of the conference were then sent by Benjamin Lwoki to the foreign ministers of Britain and Egypt, and the governor-general and prime minister of Sudan. Lwoki's letter presented federalism as *the condition* on which Southerners would agree to a united independent Sudan. If Northerners could not agree to federation, then the alternative would be a divided Sudan, using the model of the division of Pakistan from India. Lwoki's letter carried a warning concerning the South's right to self-determination, "Should a situation arise that Southern self-determination is denied by any person, we have the right to apply for an international hearing." Unfortunately for Sudan the resolution passed at the 1954 Juba conference was ignored, and the very fact of the conference itself has been erased from Sudan's nationalist history.

The most significant point about the 1954 conference is that it set the terms of the political debate in the South for years to come. The same arguments first presented then can be found expressed in various ways in the literature of the exile movements of the 1960s, in the 1965 Khartoum Round Table Conference, in the SPLM Manifesto of 1983, and were finally enshrined in the CPA: unity based on equality, but a final option for independence if such equality cannot be attained.

Further reading:
    Douglas H. Johnson, "The 1954 Juba conference, also known as the Both Diu conference", *Southern Sudan Post*
    Yosa Wawa's *Southern Sudanese Pursuits of Self-Determination: documents in political history*: pp. 115-37

5
THE TORIT MUTINY
AND THE END OF THE BRITISH EMPIRE

The mutiny of the Equatorial Corps of the Sudan Defence Force (SDF) at Torit, Equatoria Province, in August 1955 is an event of considerable historical importance. To many in Khartoum it was an aberration of no great significance in the triumphant evolution of Sudanese nationalism. Southern Sudanese tend to present it in heroic terms, as the beginning of a southern nationalist struggle. In Sudanese accounts of the 1955 Disturbances, whether written by northern or southern Sudanese, Britain and British officials come off rather badly. They were either bad counsellors, or duplicitous conspirators, or men of bad faith. But British records from the time (many of which are published in the Sudan volume I edited for the British Documents on the End of Empire Project) reveal a different aspect to these events: the impact of the mutiny on the process of the end of the British African empire.

Sudan's self-determination process as embodied in the Anglo-Egyptian agreement of 1953 (which was based on the All Parties agreement between Egypt and the northern parties) established a protracted procedure for self-government and self-determination in Sudan, involving elections in 1953, the formation of a Sudanese parliament with a Sudanese prime minister and cabinet under a British governor-general. Key posts in the civil administration were to be Sudanised, after which parliament would petition the co-dominal powers (Britain and Egypt) for new elections to a constituent assembly. Candidates would campaign on the issue of whether Sudan should unite with Egypt or become independent, and a new constitution would be drafted by the assembly according to the majority position.

The British government supported Sudanese independence. To their disappointment the pro-unionist National Union Party (NUP) won the elections and formed the first all-Sudanese government in 1954 under Ismail al-Azhari as prime minister. But in early 1955 the NUP abandoned its unionist position and came out in favour of independence. This change in NUP policy satisfied Britain's goal that Sudan should choose independence, but it was not welcome by Egypt, who increased their political activity in Sudan.

The political crisis in the South had been growing since the announcement of the Sudanisation plans in 1954. The NUP maintained a majority in parliament in part by winning some southern members to their side. Southerners voting as a bloc had the potential to make the difference between a government majority and a government defeat. The NUP had made a number of promises of preferential treatment for southerners in Sudanisation that were now clearly not going to be fulfilled. Following Buth Diu's 1954 Juba conference, which opted for Sudanese independence and a federal constitution, Azhari responded by announcing minor alterations in southern pay scales and promotions. This did not alleviate southern dissatisfaction, and in April 1955 several southern members of the NUP denounced their own government's southern policy, came out in favour of federation, and left the party. In the same month it was reported that the Egyptians were now attempting to bribe southern MPs to support a constitutional link with Egypt, and throughout the early summer of 1955 northern officials in the South reported widespread Egyptian political propaganda. Talk of federalism was on the increase, and another all-southern conference was held in Juba in July.

But the attention of politicians in Khartoum was focused elsewhere. A self-determination motion, raising the possibility of an independence plebiscite replacing elections to a constituent assembly, was passed unanimously by both houses of parliament on 16 August. Britain informed Egypt that they would accept a plebiscite if the majority of Sudanese so wished.

By this time events in the South were forcing themselves on the attention of Khartoum, Cairo and London, nearly derailing the whole process of Sudanese independence. There had been civil unrest around Yambio and Nzara in July. A mutiny plot among southern Sudanese soldiers at Torit, the headquarters of the Equatorial Corps of the Sudan Defence Force (SDF), was uncovered on 6 August, but despite this advance warning nothing was done to stop it and the mutiny broke out on 18 August. The governor-general, Sir Knox Helm, was on home leave, and the acting governor-general, William Luce, a former deputy governor of Equatoria Province, proclaimed a state of emergency in the three southern provinces in order to allow Azhari's government to deal with the emergency without reference to the co-dominal governments. Very soon after the first reports of the mutiny were received in London and Cairo the Egyptian government proposed a joint Anglo-Egyptian military intervention to restore order in the South. This was rejected by Britain.

Opinions differed about the instigation and extent of the revolt. Northern Sudanese generally attributed the mutiny solely to Egyptian agitation. Luce, one of the few British administrators to have held senior positions in both the North and the South, was of a different opinion. The mutiny, he wired London, was "symptomatic of the major internal political problem of the Sudan i.e. the relationship between the North and the South", which could be settled only by the Sudanese themselves and would require a fundamental reappraisal by the North of its attitude towards the South. The immediate problem in Khartoum was "to get Azhari and his Ministers to understand that this is anything more than a mutiny of troops". Given the obvious pro-British sentiment of so many in the South, British advice, even if based on a more intimate knowledge of the region, was suspect to the new Sudan government.

After working out a plan with Helm (who had returned to Khartoum) and Azhari, Luce went to Torit to negotiate and observe the surrender of the mutineers. Very few came in, the majority fleeing to the bush or crossing into Uganda. With the immediate crisis of the mutiny over, the chief task was to restore civil calm in the South. But Helm found Azhari uncommunicative, complacent and detached from the details of reasserting administrative control in the South, and Helm doubted both Azhari's commitment to the work of reconciliation and his own ability to influence events.

Far from postponing Sudanese independence (as Egypt hoped), the immediate effect of the Torit mutiny was for Britain to accelerate that process. The main question was whether this could best be done through a plebiscite or a direct declaration of independence.

Helm argued against a plebiscite as too difficult to implement in the wake of the disturbances in the South and urged the Foreign Office to persuade Egypt to participate in a joint recognition of independence, and the drafting of a new constitution by parliament "while the south is still quiet". He pressed hard for rapid British withdrawal, stating in September, "For me the moral is crystal clear, namely that the sooner we can get out of these almost unlimited commitments, without accompanying powers, the better".

Helm continued to argue this point, claiming that "from every point of view I can see nothing but advantages in H.M. Government divesting themselves of their Condominium responsibilities and liabilities at the earliest possible moment. If they cannot do so in agreement with Egypt then I suggest that other means should be found." After much argument back and forth between the embassy in Cairo and the Foreign Office in London Helm was instructed to inform Azhari that Her Majesty's Government would respond to an initiative from the Sudanese parliament. Britain's desire to extract itself from Sudan in the aftermath of the southern disturbances now overrode earlier commitments to constitutional procedures.

Azhari was informed in October of the United Kingdom's willingness to agree to an independence resolution passed by parliament. After much political horse-trading between the political parties in Sudan both houses of parliament passed independence motions by 22 December, and set 1 January 1956 as the date for independence.

So, how did the Torit Mutiny hasten the end of empire, not just in Sudan, but in Africa? The lesson Sir Knox Helm drew from events, not only in Sudan, but in Uganda, then still a British colony but now having to make independent decisions on how to deal with a refugee crisis generated by events in Sudan, was that after a certain point along the road to independence the dominant colonial power had little control over unfolding of events. If they were to go, then it was best they went quickly. The Foreign Office, not the Colonial Office, had responsibility for Sudan, and who was the British foreign secretary at the time of the Torit Mutiny? Harold Macmillan. It was Macmillan, as British prime minister, who, less than half a decade later announced, "the wind of change is blowing through this continent, and whether we like it or not, this growth of national consciousness is a political fact. We must all accept it as a fact, and our national policies must take account of it." It was Macmillan who accelerated Britain's decolonization of Africa. Once Britain decided to go, it decided that it was best they went quickly.

Further reading:
    Douglas H. Johnson (ed.), *Sudan, 1951-1956*

6
WHEN SOUTH SUDANESE BECAME REFUGEES

Many generations of South Sudanese have experienced life as refugees, whether exiled to foreign countries or displaced far from their original homes. Displacement and exile is a recurring theme in South Sudan's history, especially with the expansion of slavery in the nineteenth century. But the two civil wars of the late twentieth century between them created a new exodus that rivalled anything that went before. The first large-scale refugee flow in the twentieth century occurred in August 1955, shortly after the disturbances in Torit, Yambio and Yei. The sudden arrival of so many South Sudanese crossing their border caused consternation within the governments of Uganda and the United Kingdom and led to a change in the refugee law in East Africa.

Following the outbreak of the disturbances in South Sudan on 18 August 1955, refugees started appearing in Uganda as early as 20 August, some arriving in Aba, and one hundred thirty-six Equatorial Corps mutineers surrendering at Oraba. Very soon more refugees began crossing at other points: South Sudanese civilians, Christian missionaries, even a few fleeing Sudan Defence Force officers. More were expected as the crisis continued, especially if, as Ugandan administrators feared, the suppression of the mutiny was accompanied by reprisals against civilians.

This confronted the colonial officials of Uganda with both a legal and a moral dilemma. In 1914 Uganda and Sudan, both then under British administration, had enacted reciprocal legislation for the apprehension and extradition of each other's fugitive criminals who crossed over the border. Technically the "Fugitive Offenders from the Sudan Ordinance" should have come automatically into effect to send at least the mutineers back to Sudan. Quite apart from what to do about the civilian refugees who had not been actively involved in the disturbances, it now seemed impossible to deal with the mutineers under the terms of this old law.

The governor of Uganda, Sir Andrew Cohen, explained his government's reasoning to the Colonial Secretary back in London, "We are, of course, anxious to do nothing to embarrass the Sudanese Government in their difficulties and, indeed, by disarming this body of troops and taking them under our control, we have relieved them of a substantial embarrassment. At the same time we must consider the serious reaction which might be caused among our own Northern population (who are allied to many Southerners) and among troops of the 4th K.A.R., most of whom are Northerners, if the Southern troops or others were handed over generally to the Sudanese authorities." For this reason Southern troops who surrendered their arms had been told that they would not be arbitrarily returned to Sudan.

New legislation had to be drafted quickly to meet the new situation. The Sudanese government was to be informed only after the legislation was enacted and were to be told that it had been done "in order that there shall be no piece-meal extraditions but that any extraditions which there are should take place under arrangements to be agreed to between the two Governments after it has been possible fully to consider the whole position when order has been restored."

The majority of mutineers fled into the bush or across to Uganda when the mutiny collapsed. As more refugees flowed into Arua, Oraba and Gulu, and as the Ugandan government and Colonial Office debated the terms of the new legislation, the British officials in the governor-general's office in Khartoum continued to press Uganda to detain the mutineers until such time as the Sudan government could take them over. The Foreign Office in London reassured Khartoum that the mutineers would be retained, but Cohen insisted that Uganda had an obligation not to return the mutineers to Sudan against their will. At best, he suggested, the mutineers might be allowed to return to their families in Sudan "in driblets".

The Foreign Office was appalled by this suggestion. "It is one thing to give asylum to 'political refugees' who dare not go back to their own country," one official minuted, "and another to connive at and even facilitate the surreptitious return to their own country of people who have mutinied and even committed crimes. I should like to know whether the lawyers consider that the Government of Uganda could defend themselves against an accusation of unfriendly action towards the Sudan Government in giving shelter to and facilitating the return of dissident elements." Another official saw it rather differently, noting that Uganda might be accused of being "jointly involved in a conspiracy as accessories to kill murderers."

Meanwhile, the longer the former mutineers were detained in camps with no resolution as to their fate, the more restless they became. There were reports of indiscipline and the provincial commissioner feared that it would soon be impossible to hold them. In the meantime Cohen's own position had evolved, and a month after the disturbances had begun he wrote, "Our present view is that those mutineers who are unwilling to return and are not returnable under arrangements to be made, should be released from camp and allowed, if they wish, to settle freely in Uganda. But final decision depends on numbers involved."

Uganda's response to the refugee crisis, fully endorsed by the Colonial Office, caused considerable strain between Khartoum, London and Entebbe. The governor-general's office was particularly concerned that the Sudanese did not see a distinction between the colonial government in Uganda and the British government in London and were convinced that there was a British plot to side with the mutineers. While many in the Foreign Office were inclined to give full support to Khartoum's demands for extradition, there were others who saw broader international implications in the politics between two incipient independent African states. The senior legal advisor pointed out that Britain itself faced possible asylum claims from potential risings in Eastern Europe, then under the domination of Soviet Russia, and asked how a massive repatriation of the Sudanese mutineers might set "a precedent in the future" in Africa and elsewhere. From general principles he argued that Britain could not force wholesale extraditions. In addition to that was the fact that Britain was partially responsible for the political set up in Sudan. "Is it", he asked, "indeed, justice to look at this revolt in isolation and approach the problem with the idea that we must 'try to find some method of returning these men to the Sudanese authorities'?" Harold Macmillan, then foreign secretary with responsibility for Sudan, recorded that he was "shaken" by these arguments.

In October Khartoum sent two Sudan Defence Force officers to Uganda to report on the possibility of extraditing the mutineers, and they returned with a nominal roll of some one hundred forty mutineers then gathered in Gulu. In the meantime Khartoum also requested Uganda to supply a complete list of names of civilians who had crossed into Uganda. The Ugandan government urged Khartoum to send their applications for extradition soon, and to agree that all those not facing extradition should be released.

A few ex-mutineers who had escaped detention in Gulu had been apprehended and arrested on crossing into Sudan. This gave Governor-General Sir Knox Helm the idea "whether honour would not be satisfied if it were amicably arranged that the Sudan Government had, say, one week's notice of the date on which internees would either be freed or allowed to escape, and could make their dispositions accordingly." The Foreign Office gave him permission to put this suggestion to the Sudanese prime minister, Ismail el-Azhari.

Extradition applications finally came from Khartoum in December, but on examination most of the forty-five names listed were not among those in detention in Gulu. The government concluded that the majority were either not present in Uganda, or, if present, their whereabouts were unknown. There were further problems with the extradition warrants in that the evidence in them appeared to the Ugandan government to be insufficient, and none been signed by a magistrate. In the end Uganda decided to release all members of the Equatorial Corps not subject to extradition proceedings. How many might have returned surreptitiously to Sudan is not known. Most stayed in Uganda; some settled permanently.

Uganda became a significant haven for refugees and exiles in the 1960s when the civil war began in earnest. The precedents set in 1955 created a new legal context for refugees in East Africa, establishing a clear criteria for extraditable, as opposed to political offences, and paved the way for the later, larger, influx of South Sudanese refugees to have the same level of protection refugees in European countries were then being afforded.

Further reading:
    Douglas H. Johnson (ed.), *Sudan, 1951-1956*

7
JUST HOW DID SUDAN GAIN ITS INDEPENDENCE?

The date of Sudan's independence, 1 January 1956, has achieved a status of double importance. Not only does it mark the date of Sudan's emergence as a nation, but by its inclusion in the both the Addis Ababa and Comprehensive Peace Agreements it also defines the outline of the southern Sudan. But just how did Sudan get its independence on this date?

By 1953 Sudan was set on a ponderous and protracted procedure, defined by the Anglo-Egyptian Agreement, which was supposed to lead from self-government to self-determination. It involved two sets of national elections: the first to the Legislative Assembly in 1953, the second to a future Constituent Assembly. The first elections were to lead to the formation of a Sudanese parliament under a Sudanese prime minister and cabinet (all under a British governor-general and British constitutional advisers), and the Sudanisation of the civil service, police, army and other national institutions. The second elections were supposed to lead to the passing of a national constitution that would either bind Sudan in union with Egypt, or release it as an independent state. Only then would the Anglo-Egyptian Condominium be dissolved.

It didn't quite work out that way, and the reason was because of events in the South. A question arises: if the British were so keen to depart from Sudan before constitutional issues could be resolved because of the Southern Disturbances, could southern parliamentarians have leveraged a better deal for themselves as a price of this early departure?

Shortly after the Anglo-Egyptian Agreement was signed a British minister defined British objectives in Sudan as ensuring that Sudan chose independence, that the South got "a fair deal", and that the transfer of power "should take place with dignity and goodwill". The election of a pro-Egyptian National Union

Party (NUP) government under Ismail al-Azhari as prime minister in 1954 was a disappointment for Britain, but it was Egypt's turn to be disappointed when in 1955 the NUP switched from supporting Egyptian union to Sudanese independence. For Britain this policy switch satisfied one objective in ensuring Sudan chose independence. It remained to get the South "a fair deal" and to leave with "dignity and goodwill."

With the conversion of the NUP to the cause of independence there were moves in parliament "to eliminate self-determination". The Ummah Party, which had been willing to tear up the 1953 agreement after failing in the elections, now proposed to dispense with the self-determination process "on the ground that the whole country is agreed upon independence". Failing that, they wished to replace elections to a constituent assembly with a plebiscite on independence. The idea of a plebiscite had been floated at different times by the Ummah, Azhari and the Egyptians. Azhari now resisted the idea of a plebiscite, but in July Sayyid Ali al-Mirghani of the Khatmiyya sect (patron of the NUP) supported it.

The self-determination process formally began when the Sudanisation Committee reported on 2 August 1955 that its task was completed. A self-determination motion was debated in the House of Representatives on 16 August, in which the possibility of a plebiscite was mentioned, and both houses of parliament unanimously passed the resolution. Both Sayyid Abd al-Rahman al-Mahdi of the Ansar (patron of the Ummah Party) and Sayyid Ali al-Mirghani now publicly supported a plebiscite, and Britain informed the Egyptian government that Britain would accept it if the majority of Sudanese so wished.

But the Torit Mutiny intervened, and nearly derailed the independence process. In fact, it *did* derail the agreed self-determination process by which Sudanese were supposed to pass a constitution before the Condominium was dissolved. Independence was achieved, but at the expense of self-determination, because in the end no vote was put to the Sudanese people as a whole, and independence was decided by a parliament who *exceeded their mandate*. How did this happen?

While the mutiny in the South was being suppressed Britain and Egypt agreed in advance to accept a plebiscite should the Sudanese parliament vote in favour of one, which it did at the end of August. Support for an outright declaration of independence by Sudan now came from a variety of corners. Nasser contemplated a unilateral recognition of Sudanese independence as a means of salvaging some of Egypt's influence following the backlash against its Sudan policy after the Torit Mutiny, for which it was being blamed. Britain's Colonial Office supported Britain's unilateral recognition of Sudanese independence for the opposite reason: to forestall the advance of Egyptian influence towards East Africa. Sir Knox Helm, the British governor-general, urged the Foreign Office to persuade Egypt to participate in a joint recognition of independence and a parliamentary drafting of a new constitution, "while the south is still quiet". On this last point Helm was at odds with the Foreign Office, who were then of the view that parliament had *no mandate* to settle constitutional issues.

Egypt's Nasser now began to resist British pressure to accelerate self-determination, arguing against altering the self-determination procedures. He eventually accepted a plebiscite, but not a declaration of independence. Cold War politics now intervened to alter political calculations. Egypt signed an agreement with Czechoslovakia to purchase Soviet Bloc weapons in October, and this removed Britain's last inhibition against offending Egypt over Sudan. Britain's foreign secretary, Harold Macmillan, instructed Helm to inform Azhari that Britain was willing to recognise Sudanese independence immediately.

Predictably, the embassy in Cairo argued against unilateral action, citing the possible repudiation of the Suez Canal base agreement in retaliation, but the Foreign Office and Macmillan saw the initiative over Sudan as a way of showing Nasser that Britain would not "accept tamely a defeat of the kind he has administered us" with the Czech arms deal. The only concession to Cairo was the instruction to Helm to inform Azhari that Her Majesty's Government would merely "respond" to an initiative from the Sudanese parliament. The Foreign Office had apparently forgotten its own prescient warning back in 1953 that a declaration of independence, even by a large majority of both houses of parliament, would be likely to create discontent among minorities and pave the way for civil war.

Azhari was so informed on 12 October 1955. He at first saw no need for a hurried resolution, and it was Helm who pressed him. Azhari's hesitation stemmed from splits within his own party, leading to a vote of no confidence, and an opposition demand that a coalition "national" government should supervise the drafting of the constitution. When the southern representatives of the Liberal Party declared that they were not prepared to discuss Sudan's future in parliament, the Foreign Office was dismayed that this boycott could undermine their justification for cutting short self-determination. The southern parliamentarians were thus in a stronger position to extract concessions from the Foreign Office than they realised, and had they but known this they might have been able to get more favourable terms for the South in the subsequent independence motion.

In the midst of parliamentary deadlock in Sudan, renewed concern for a fair deal for the South was expressed in both houses of parliament in Britain. William Luce, the former deputy governor of Equatoria and the constitutional affairs adviser who had been acting governor-general at the time of the Torit Mutiny, reassured the Foreign Office that the question of the South could not be settled independently of the constitutional questions for the entire country. Since a plebiscite would address only the issue of independence from Egypt, whose outcome was now considered a foregone conclusion, and not the internal constitutional structure of Sudan, it was far better, he declared, to get past the formula for independence and on to the real issues confronting the country. A national government, which he felt likely would replace the NUP government, would be bound to treat the South generously.

It was precisely to avoid the creation of a national government that Azhari finally tabled the independence motions, and then only after Helm had returned to Britain on Christmas leave. The wording of the resolutions requested the governor-general to ask the co-domini to recognise Sudanese independence forthwith. A constituent assembly was promised after independence and, in response the demands from the Liberal Party, federation for the South would be given "serious consideration". The motions were passed by the House on 19 December and the Senate on 22 December, but the date of 1 January 1956 for independence was decided only on 27 December. Helm was requested not to return to Sudan for the independence ceremonies.

Of Britain's three objectives Sudan's independence was obtained, but at the expense of a "fair deal" for the South, and with only the semblance of "dignity and goodwill". Sudan achieved its independence, but the Sudanese people as a whole were denied self-determination. The Foreign Office's forgotten prediction that a parliamentary declaration of independence would pave the way for civil war would come true all too soon.

Further reading:
    Douglas H. Johnson (ed.), *Sudan, 1951-1956*

8
HOW LONG DID SUDAN'S FIRST CIVIL WAR LAST?

How long did Sudan's first civil war last? Most people will say seventeen years, from the Torit Mutiny in August 1955 to the Addis Ababa Agreement in February 1972. These are the generally accepted dates of that war, but as with so many generally accepted historical "facts" the truth is not so clear-cut. For some time now historians have questioned this assumption, though their scepticism has yet to be shared by journalists, politicians, and the South Sudanese public alike. Is this just academic nit-picking? If everyone believes that South Sudan's struggle for independence began in 1955, and South Sudanese fought continuously for seventeen years, why should a few historians question it? The answer, of course, is that it is important to understand how South Sudan has got to where it is today, to know that there were different ways of struggling, and different avenues for Sudan to follow.

What happened in August 1955? On August 18 a mutiny broke out among the headquarters troops of the Equatorial Corps in Torit. This was followed by a succession of small mutinies within the army, police and prison service in Kapoeta, Juba, Terekeka, Yei, Meridi, Yambio, Nzara and Malakal, but these outbreaks were more a reaction to the news from Torit than a co-ordinated rebellion. The mutineers presented no clear manifesto, no demand was made for southern independence, and there was no organized attempt to mobilize the general populace behind any political platform. Aside from a shoot-out with prison warders in Malakal Upper Nile was quiet. In Wau police inspector Gordon Muortat and other southern administrators persuaded the northern governor and senior staff to leave the province, which they kept under control. Northern troops were flown to Equatoria, William Luce, a former deputy governor of Equatoria and one of the few remaining British officials in Khartoum, negotiated the surrender of some of the mutineers, but the majority fled either to Uganda or the bush. The disturbances were over before the end of August.

One political outcome of the August disturbances was that Sudanese independence and the withdrawal of the former condominium powers was accelerated while internal constitutional discussions were deferred (chapter 5). There followed what turned out to be a brief period of parliamentary government, during which there was no fighting in the South (aside from a few clashes with dispersed mutineers living in the bush), but a great deal of political activity in Khartoum. This was a time when people like Benjamin Lwoki, Paulo Logali, Stanislaus Paysama, Joseph Oduho, Fr. Saturnino Lohure and Buth Diu in Khartoum, and Abd al-Rahman Sule and others in Juba, Wau and Malakal took the lead in defining the South's political position and options.

With Sudanese independence an established fact, arguments turned towards the form of constitutional government that would best protect the South's interests. Southern MPs proposed a federal system, but when this was "considered" and rejected by a parliamentary committee in 1956 southern politicians re-organized themselves around the federal issue in the first post-independence elections in 1957. Elections were fought less along party lines and more around the proposal to support a federal constitution. A large majority of pro-federalist southern MPs was returned, forming a substantial Federal Bloc in parliament. In addition to this the southern parliamentarians began to reach out beyond the territorial constituency of the South to MPs from the other marginal areas of the east, the Nuba Mountains and Darfur. Federalism was no longer just a southern project but was gaining support in other parts of the nation. This is one of the reasons why the military seized power in 1958, to save the country from "falling apart".

The military government of General Ibrahim Abboud introduced the policy of basing national unity on the twin principles of

Arabism and Islam. It also equated federalism with separatism and outlawed any discussion of it. This closed down any possibility of a national political dialogue on the constitutional future of the country. It also made southern ex-parliamentarians particular targets of police surveillance and harassment. Southern civil servants and students also became visible targets of Arabization and proselytization. It was at this point that southern leaders began to go into exile rather than face arrest, schools were closed and students, too, faced the choice of arrest or flight, especially after widespread school strikes in the South in 1962. Those students who did not go into exile went to the bush where they joined the remnants of the 1955 mutineers.

There was now a substantial southern Sudanese exile and refugee population living in neighbouring countries, particularly the Congo and Uganda. The exiles were joined by such former parliamentarians as Joseph Oduho and Fr. Saturnino Lohure, as well as such civil administrators as William Deng. The exiles were no longer just groups of refugees. They now had a leadership that could begin to organize political activity and articulate a political programme for them.

1962 saw the formation of the first exile political movement, the Sudan African Closed District National Union (later shortened to SANU). This was followed in 1963 by the first organized military activity of guerrilla units answering to the name of 'Anyanya' (poison, or snake venom). SANU drew its lessons from the successful East African nationalist parties, TANU in what was then Tanganyika and KANU in Kenya, and sent petitions to the UN and the newly formed OAU to draw attention to its cause. The Anyanya took longer to organize as a truly pan-southern force. With no regular source of supply guerrilla units tended to operate independently of each other in the field. The overthrow of Abboud in 1964 paradoxically gave the Anyanya their first real access to arms, when Khartoum decided to ship arms to the Simba rebels in the Congo. It was the Anyanya, then in control of the Congolese border, who seized the arms, making them a far more potent military force than they had previously been. The failure of the Round Table talks in Khartoum and the massacres in Juba, Wau and other parts of the southern Sudan in 1965 accelerated the momentum of a war that would not end until 1972.

By this reckoning Sudan's first civil war, marked by an active exile movement and an organized insurgency, lasted no more than a decade, from 1962 to 1972. Why is it important to emphasise this fact? Doesn't it just undervalue South Sudan's struggle for independence (which some now even want to claim began in 1820)?

The answer to this criticism is that it is important to understand the evolution of the struggle, to understand that there were different options at different times, that there were different choices to be made. It is important to understand, for instance, why Gordon Muortat chose to adhere to his policeman's duty to maintain law and order in 1955 rather than join a spontaneous but disorganized rising, yet a decade later he had become an outstanding advocate for southern independence, a position he maintained throughout the period of the Addis Ababa peace and after. Or why Joseph Oduho and Fr. Saturnino Lohure, both participants in parliamentary democracy and advocates of a united federal Sudan, became exile insurgents, fighting for southern separation.

There was a window of opportunity in the mid-1950s when the country's constitutional future could be debated freely, when Sudan's leaders collectively could have opted for a political framework that might have avoided war and maintained national unity. That window was closed by a military coup. By the time another window was opened with the overthrow of the military dictatorship civil war had begun and both that window and the length of time it remained open were narrowed.

The decade of the first civil war can be seen as part of a continuum of a broader political struggle within Sudan, one that embraces not just South Sudanese but other marginalized peoples. Different generations of South Sudanese have had to try parliamentary politics, single party politics, war and negotiation before finally settling on and achieving the goal of national independence.

9
THE TRIAL OF *THE VIGILANT* AND PRESS FREEDOM IN SUDAN

I remember when I first learned of the Juba and Wau massacres in 1965 from a copy of the American weekly *Newsweek*. I was of an age when I began to take a serious interest in news, and the tide of African independence was then one of the big international news stories. I also thought I knew something about Sudan from reading British imperial history and African exploration. So the story immediately caught my eye, but it also puzzled me. This was the first report I ever read about a civil war in Sudan, as none of my previous reading had hinted at this unhappy story of violence.

What I did not know at the time was that the reason the event was reported in an international journal like *Newsweek* was because of the efforts of African journalists to break the story. Chief among these were journalists of *The Vigilant*, the newly established newspaper of the Southern Front party in Sudan. What didn't get reported in the international press was the Sudan government's attempt to suppress the story and shut down that paper. This story is still untold, but it is a story that needs telling.

In 1965 Sudan was just emerging from seven years of military dictatorship. The government of General Ibrahim Abboud had shut down parliament, banned political parties and an independent press, declared federation for the South to be subversive, and targeted the educated minority of southern students and civil servants. During this time exile southern political movements and an organized insurgency in the South began, turning sporadic violence into an escalating civil war.

Abboud's overthrow in October 1964 opened a brief window of opportunity for a political resolution in the South. New parties emerged, among them the Southern Front. The transitional government called a cease-fire and convened a Round Table Conference in Khartoum in March. The conference failed to come up with any solutions, the cease fire ended, and national elections for a Constituent Assembly were held, from which much of the South was excluded because of insecurity. In June the new Assembly passed a resolution authorizing the government to "restore law and order" in the South and give the security forces a "free hand". This was the background to the events of July.

On 8 and 9 July 1965 shooting broke out in Juba as a party of about seventy soldiers combed through the main residential areas of the town attacking people in private houses, in church buildings, and in the general hospital. Two days later, on 11 July 1965, a wedding party in Wau was also attacked by Sudanese soldiers. The full number of killed in both massacres was never formally established. Reports ranged from at least seventy-six in Wau and some 360 in Juba to a total of over a thousand for both incidents. Even the Khartoum Arabic press reported over 400 deaths in Juba alone.

One of the first papers to publish accounts of these events was *The Vigilant*. The government response was swift: it seized issues of the paper and closed it down. The strategic importance of silencing *The Vigilant* was that as an English language newspaper it was widely read by the diplomatic community in Khartoum; thus giving them access to a version of events which contradicted the official line that those killed in Juba and Wau were insurgents.

The government then accused *The Vigilant*'s proprietor, Darius Bashir, editor, Bona Malwal, and assistant editor, Chan Malual Chan, of inciting hatred against classes, illegal opposition to the government, and disturbance of the peace. The offending articles produced as evidence included those on the two massacres, others about conditions in the southern Sudan and Nuba Mountains, and one entitled "Ours is a Liberation

Movement", written by a young lawyer, Ambrose Riny (later the first chief justice in the post-2005 Government of Southern Sudan).

The paper was defended by Abel Alier, a former judge and leading member of the Southern Front. His strategy was to establish the truth of the reports, which he did by calling as witnesses two northern officials and several survivors of the massacres.

The two northern witnesses were senior officials in Ministries in Khartoum who testified they had received official notification of the disturbing news of the death of some of their departments' employees in the Wau massacre. The testimony of these two government officials helped to establish that at least some of the claims in *The Vigilant* were not southern inventions, but could be verified through official sources.

The most telling evidence was presented by witnesses to the killings in Wau, Juba and Yei. Three Dinka school mistresses had been guests at the wedding. All three testified to the identity of their attackers. Mary Ayat, from Aweil, described how the house in Wau had been surrounded by government soldiers who then opened fire. When the prosecuting attorney challenged her identification of government soldiers the president of the court intervened, saying, "Are there any others in this country besides government soldiers?" And when the prosecutor also challenged Mary Ayat's knowledge of Arabic, the court president then conversed with her in Arabic and announced, "Oh, she speaks good Arabic," a remark loudly applauded by the court spectators. Abel Alier then asked her if the soldiers also spoke English, Jur, Dinka or any other southern languages, to which she replied no.

Rachel Adak John, who was then nineteen years old, confirmed the identity of the soldiers and what they said to each other. The prosecutor unwisely tried to shake her testimony by asking,

"What was the colour of the soldiers' skin?", to which she replied, "Such as your colour," provoking laughter in court. Susan Aluel, a visiting school mistress from Tonj, corroborated the other witnesses, and again the prosecutor's cross-examination only provided more convincing details of what she saw and heard.

Dr. Noel Warile was a medical doctor on duty at Juba hospital who saw, and counted, many of the dead and wounded brought there. He witnessed government soldiers shooting civilians and was himself the target of one squad of soldiers who broke into the hospital shooting southern medical staff. Mrs. Mary Antonio Anjelo Kenyi from Yei then described in simple detail how her husband, a prison officer, was shot dead in their own home, by a corporal in the army, with the distinctive marks on his cheeks of a Sha'iqi from the North.

In their ruling the panel of three judges acquitted both the proprietor and the assistant editor and declared that none of the articles giving details of the murders in Juba, Wau, or elsewhere in the South were seditious. Only Ambrose Riny's article, "Ours is a Liberation Movement", published before the massacres, was deemed seditious, by virtue of its use of the words "revolution" and "liberation struggle", and the editor was found guilty of incitement on the basis of this article alone. Then at variance with its own ruling the court lifted the ban on *The Vigilant*, stating, "The need for media of enlightenment in this country hardly needs emphasis. Newspapers which are published in English are scanty. To ban *The Vigilant* would be to deprive non-Arabic readers of a media for spreading news and hence enlightenment."

The decision was referred to a Supreme Court Justice for confirmation. Whereas the original judges had skirted the issue of the massacres, Supreme Court Justice Abd al-Majid Imam, a Muslim of southern ancestry, faced it squarely. Criticising the original court's refusal to comment on the issues giving details of the massacres, he ruled that the facts of the Juba and Wau massacres had "been proved by abundant evidence and beyond any reasonable doubt". Commenting that an editor who brought such grave crimes to light ought to be protected rather than punished, he then confirmed that the editor's fine for publishing one seditious article would be no more than £S 20.

The trial of *The Vigilant* was extraordinary in many ways. It revealed that some Northerners were willing to testify publicly in defence of Southerners. It demonstrated the independence of the judiciary. The conviction on one article may have been tactical; for by convicting the editor on an article written before the July 1965 events, the courts may have effectively prevented the government from bringing any further prosecutions. In any case the testimony of the witnesses to the massacres went undisputed in the first judgment, and was broadcast vigorously in the confirming judgment.

When *The Vigilant* won its case, it won an historic victory on behalf of all Sudanese people and the entire Sudanese nation, a victory, however, which seems to have gone unnoticed, unrecognized and unprotected. The details of the violence in the South reported by *The Vigilant* and proven in court did not have the same impact on the northern Sudanese public as contemporary reports of US army massacres in Vietnam had on large sections of the American public, turning them against the war. Had the northern Sudanese public reacted with horror at what was being done in their name in the South, had they been roused by the massacres in Juba and Wau and the defence of *The Vigilant*, there might have been no second civil war, and Sudan might be a freer country today.

10
55 YEARS OF BANANAS?

My first visit to an African country was in 1969, when I was a student at Makerere University College in Uganda. There I met South Sudanese for the first time, and it was then that my involvement with South Sudan began. It wasn't until many years later that I was able to revisit Uganda: after Amin's dictatorship, Obote's stolen election, and the military regime of the Okellos.

My revisit coincided with the thirtieth anniversary of Uganda's independence, which Ugandans marked in a variety of imaginative ways. The National Theatre in Kampala was showing a satirical play entitled "Thirty Years of Bananas", set in the basement storeroom of the National Museum where all the statues of Uganda's past presidents were kept. The one remarkable feature of these statues was that none of them had ears – because the presidents could not hear (or would not listen to) the people. As the cover sheets were removed one by one the storekeeper – a Rwandan refugee – kept up a sardonic commentary on each one: what they had promised to do, what they had failed to do, what they had actually done, and how they ended up. It was a wildly popular play and the audiences were convulsed in laughter.

A more sober reflection on Uganda's first thirty years was broadcast on Ugandan TV, where various ordinary citizens, some who had been adults at independence, and some who were born the same year, related their experiences and gave their assessment of how those years of independence had been spent. One thirty year-old man concluded the programme with this question, "So, we got our self-determination. How did we use it?"

In the year of South Sudan's referendum Sudan celebrated fifty-five years of its independence. In that period it achieved many firsts: it was the first post-war African country to obtain independence; the first post-war independent African country to have its democratic government overthrown by a coup and replaced by a military dictatorship; the first country to oust its military rulers and restore democracy; the first country to have a second coup; the first country to have a civil war; the first country to end that civil war by negotiation; the first country to have a second civil war. During those fifty-five years many other African countries have caught up with Sudan in the number of coups and civil wars, but Sudan still holds the record for having the most firsts. It is fair to ask this question: with this record, did Sudan have fifty-five years of bananas?

In the 2011 referendum South Sudan exercised its self-determination. For many South Sudanese self-determination has often been a code word for independence. But self-determination is more than that, it is a process by which a people decide how they wish to be governed, or how they wish to govern themselves. It is not a single act; it is on-going. And for South Sudanese the process has been on-going for more than fifty-five years, at least as far back as the Juba Conference of 1954 when the Southern leadership of the day defined in broad terms the conditions on which they would accept the unity of the country, and reserving their right to self-determination if those conditions were not met.

The result of the referendum was never in doubt. South Sudan got its independence, not through negotiation with a colonial power, but by the will of its people. The euphoria was infectious. Even the most sober and sceptical outside observers found it difficult not to get caught up in the excitement. But this should also have been a time for reflection.

In the North there has been more recrimination than reflection, as different parties apportioned blame for the break-up of the country, with the NCP getting most of the blame. And indeed, pro-independence South Sudanese have much to thank the NCP for. Not just because they signed the CPA and announced they would abide by the referendum result. Their Salvation Revolution halted the peace negotiations of 1989 where Southern independence was not even an option under discussion. And by their policies since then, their conduct of the war that their intervention prolonged, and by their obstructive approach to the implementation of the CPA, they made Southern independence a certainty. When confronted with the choice between a united Sudan and their version of an Islamic state, they voted for their Islamic state, and South Sudanese voted with their feet or, more appropriately, with their open palms.

But all parties – northern and southern – who have formed governments since 1954 should also reflect on their part in Sudan getting to where it is today. What were the policies, what were the actions that combined to make unity unattractive those last fifty-five years? If South Sudanese were euphoric about getting their independence, are there any benefits of belonging to a united nation that they have had to give up? These questions are important because no geological fault-line opened up separating the South from the North on 9 July. North and South Sudan remain physically, economically, and socially linked. If people on both sides of the border can come up with honest answers for why unity failed, this, then, is the first step to coming up with answers to the pressing questions of how two newly separate nations now can coexist and succeed.

New nations always face challenges. Consider the odds against one such nation. At independence its northern neighbour, against whom it had waged war to get independence, was hostile and was stirring up trouble along the border. There were strong regional differences within the country that threatened to tear the country apart, and some states were threatening further secession. Some former freedom fighters had already rebelled. At least three different currencies were circulating within its borders, and foreign currencies were stronger than its own. It had no agreed policy on managing its debt. Its first two presidents were vilified in the press loyal to one of their ministers, who, when he later became vice-president kept up a clandestine correspondence with a foreign power that would be considered treasonous by modern standards. A minister of finance plotted an army coup, and another vice-president shot and killed the finance minister – and got away with it.

The nation, of course, was the United States of America. At independence Canada, its northern neighbour, remained under British rule and continued to support Indian resistance in the USA's northwest territories. The northern and southern states were bitterly divided over the issue of slavery and could keep the new union together only by agreeing not to discuss openly the issue that divided them. Not only did the states of Georgia and South Carolina threaten to secede if the federal government attempted to abolish slavery, but the north-eastern states of New England, who still had strong commercial ties with the mother country, also threatened to secede if their trading interests were undermined by national policies. Former revolutionary soldiers had risen up in Shays' Rebellion, also in New England. The British pound, the Spanish silver peso, and the American dollar were all used as legal tender, with the first two European currencies much stronger than the dollar. Arguments about who was responsible for the national debt were not settled for the first twelve years of the nation's existence. George Washington, the first president, was violently attacked in the press loyal to Thomas Jefferson, his secretary of state. The same press kept up these attacks on John Adams, Washington's successor, even while Jefferson was serving as Adams' vice-president. During that time Jefferson was also in secret correspondence with France to undermine Adams' foreign policy. Alexander Hamilton, the nation's first secretary of the treasury (whom South Sudanese will recognize from his picture on the ten dollar bills that used to circulate so freely here), plotted to seize power by raising and taking control of a national army. And when no longer in office he was killed in a duel by Aaron Burr,

Jefferson's former vice-president. This all took place within the first seventeen years of the United States' existence as an independent nation. It is no wonder that many European observers confidently predicted that this new nation could not possibly last.

Nations born in adverse circumstances can overcome them. But this leads us back to the question the young Ugandan asked of his own country, "So, we got our self-determination. How did we use it?" For South Sudanese that question refers immediately to the present as well as the future, rather than the past. And taking a lesson from the play, "Thirty Years of Bananas", perhaps the best way South Sudanese can make sure that they use their self-determination well is to elect leaders with ears – the bigger the better – and whatever the size of their ears to speak loudly and forcefully for a better future.

11
SUDAN AND THE COMMONWEALTH

Shortly after independence the new Republic of South Sudan announced its intention of applying for membership of the Commonwealth of Nations (formerly the British Commonwealth) This is not surprising as the Commonwealth currently includes all of Britain's former African colonies, including two states – Tanzania and South Africa – who left the Commonwealth and then returned, and even two nations – Mozambique and Rwanda – who were never part of the British Empire. It would be wholly appropriate for ROSS to join, as the first discussions concerning Sudan's possible membership of the Commonwealth back in 1951 focused on the future of the southern Sudan. But this was also one reason why Sudan, the first African country to gain independence after World War II, never joined the Commonwealth.

To understand why Sudan did not join the Commonwealth we must remember first that Sudan was not a British colony. It was an Egyptian colony, administered by Britain under the terms of the Anglo-Egyptian Treaty. In the diplomatic competition between those two countries over Sudan's future Egypt was determined to remove Britain from Sudan, while Britain was equally determined to keep Egypt out. Second, the Commonwealth itself was a new creation, originally composed of what were then known as the "White Dominions" (Canada, Australia, New Zealand and – ironically – South Africa), and while India and Pakistan were too large and important to exclude from the Commonwealth when they became independent after the war, there was no guarantee that smaller, "all black" nations would be welcome.

Britain had conceded Sudan's right to self-government, self-determination and independence as early as 1947, and in the Anglo-Egyptian tug-of-war that followed it tried to balance keeping northern Sudanese nationalists on their side by progressively introducing self-government, and reassuring southern Sudanese that self-government and self-determination would not lead to their ultimate marginalization. Throughout 1951 both the Foreign Office and the Sudan government were committed to maintaining some sort of constitutional safeguards for the South, allowing for the retention of British administrative staff there later than elsewhere in Sudan. When Egypt unilaterally abrogated both the Condominium Agreement and the Anglo-Egyptian Treaty, the legal instruments underpinning Britain's administration of Sudan, the governor-general suggested that Commonwealth membership for Sudan might allow for the appointment of a British high commissioner as a trustee for the South while the rest of the country became self-governing.

Egypt's abrogation of the treaty not only accelerated constitutional and political developments in Sudan, but it also provoked a debate within the different branches of the British government about future relations within the colonial empire and the Commonwealth. The prospect of early Sudanese self-determination now forced them to debate seriously the issue of expanding membership of the Commonwealth to non-settler African territories. The immediate reaction of the Foreign and Commonwealth Relations Offices to the governor-general's proposal to admit Sudan into the Commonwealth was that such a proposal would risk South Africa, whose National Party government under D.F. Malan had recently introduced apartheid, leaving the Commonwealth.

In suggesting the possibility of a two-tiered membership, with something short of dominion status for the less important territories, the Colonial Office tried to separate the developments in Sudan from the rest of the empire. There were others in the government who wished to push the issue on behalf of Sudan. Douglas Dodds-Parker, a former Sudan administrator turned Conservative member of parliament (and who later served as parliamentary under-secretary in both the Foreign and

Commonwealth Relations Offices), put forward the case for Sudanese membership of the Commonwealth and, noting that many colonial territories were watching closely Her Majesty's Government's arrangements for Sudan, urged an examination of the implications of such membership for the rest of the empire. It was an issue that received increasing attention throughout 1952 and into 1953.

At the end of 1952 Britain's prime minister, Sir Anthony Eden posed the question of allowing Sudan to apply for membership of the Commonwealth should it choose independence. The issue being raised, it had to be considered. The Commonwealth Relations Office produced a paper that deferred the question of Sudan's admission to the Commonwealth until such time as a more detailed position paper concerning Commonwealth membership of other "more important" colonial territories, the Gold Coast (later Ghana) in particular, could be drafted. Having argued vigorously against the pace of Sudan's progress towards self-government and self-determination, the Colonial Office now appeared to be much more in favour of the idea of Sudan joining the Commonwealth than either the Foreign or Commonwealth Relations Offices. One Colonial Office official commented that the Foreign Office "seem to be moved by the desire to get shot of the Sudan, in the interests of easy relationships with Egypt", while the Commonwealth Relations Office were motivated "by fear of anything which is going to cause awkwardness with Dr. Malan". He expressed a worry about the possible negative effect on public opinion in the West African territories if the arguments for excluding Sudan were made public. Another official agreed, further alleging that the Foreign Office "underrate both the strategic importance of the Sudan and...the degree of psychological influence which members of the Commonwealth can exercise on a country's behaviour."

Ultimately the Foreign Office decided that any appearance of pressing for Sudanese membership would be misrepresented by

Egypt, and possibly misunderstood in Sudan as an attempt to maintain British control over the country. For this reason no active measures were taken to encourage the Sudanese to apply.

One outcome of this tortuous debate between the different ministries of the British government was that it aired the arguments for opening the Commonwealth to the membership of "non-white" African territories, and helped pave the way for the inclusion, first of Ghana and Nigeria, and ultimately the rest of British Africa. South Africa did withdraw from the Commonwealth as the tide of African independence grew, but rejoined after achieving majority rule. Whether Sudan's domestic politics would have been greatly affected by Commonwealth membership is open to debate. But the whole issue has now come full circle: Commonwealth membership having first been proposed specifically to benefit the South, South Sudan now has an opportunity to make that choice on its own.

Further reading:
    Douglas H. Johnson (ed.), *Sudan, 1951-1956*

12
FRIENDS AND NEIGHBOURS

On July 9th 2011 South Sudan officially became independent and hosted a ceremony attended by numerous heads of state and their representatives, all (or almost all) declaring their lasting friendship for the new republic. There are certainly a number of governments who assisted in both the peace negotiations and the implementation of the peace agreement that led to South Sudanese self-determination and independence. But as Lord Palmerston, Britain's mid-nineteenth-century foreign secretary and prime minister, famously said, "Nations have no permanent friends or allies, they only have permanent interests." We can see how this applies to South Sudan if we recall the history of Sudan's twenty-two year civil war.

It is important to remember that when the war began in 1983 the United States was on the side of Khartoum, and remained on Khartoum's side, no matter who was in power, for the first ten years of the war. There were two main reasons for this consistent support: Sudan under Nimeiri was one of the few regional governments to endorse the Camp David Agreement between Israel and Egypt, and Sudan was on the front line of the Cold War, opposed both by the Marxist regime in Ethiopia and America's enemy in Libya, Muamar Qaddafi. As long as those conditions remained, whatever regime operated in Khartoum had some measure of military and economic support from Washington.

I was in Malakal when war broke out in May 1983 (little knowing that the future president of the Republic of South Sudan, Salva Kiir Mayardit, was also then in Malakal and one of the covert organizers of what became the SPLA). It had been obvious that war was coming ever since Nimeiri dissolved the Southern Regional Government in 1981 and replaced it with military rulers under General Rassas. Many Southerners I knew worried about where the South would get its international support in the coming war. Some bemoaned the fact that the collaboration of South Sudanese in Amin's regime closed post-Amin Uganda to them. Others hoped that the Camp David agreement would fail so that they could renew Israeli support, which had been so important towards the end of the first civil war. The only regional allies left were Mengistu's Ethiopia and Qaddafi's Libya, and it is not surprising that these became the SPLA's first significant patrons.

I tried to explain this to representatives of the US government, first in the embassy in Khartoum, and later at a hearing of the Congressional Sub-Committee on Africa, but policy considerations overrode any deep analysis of Sudanese internal politics. As far as the US Defense Department was concerned the SPLA was a Soviet proxy, and Hassan al-Tourabi had many fans in the State Department. There was the general feeling that if the SPLA were shorn of its external supporters, the war would very quickly end. So, Vice-President George Herbert Walker Bush visited Khartoum with prominent evangelical Christian leaders in his entourage, Washington accepted Khartoum's line that only 3% of the South was outside government control and blocked relief aid to non-government areas, and Khartoum and Washington both gave support to what US President Reagan termed the Ethiopian "Contras", borrowing a name from US-supported Central American guerrillas.

Of course after Nimeiri fell Libya immediately switched its support back to Khartoum. When later Mengistu fell and the SPLA evacuated out of Ethiopia the war continued for another eleven years, its underlying issues unresolved. The end of the Cold War changed Washington's priorities in the region, and a new administration gave its support to the leaders of the "African Renaissance" in Uganda, Ethiopia and Eritrea. When these countries, becoming alarmed by Tourabi's expansionist designs against them, began to back the SPLA, and as "Islamist terrorism" came to be perceived as the next great threat to the West, Washington, too, realigned its support to the SPLA. This did not translate into endorsement of an independent South: that was not yet the SPLA's stated primary goal, though Ugandan, Ethiopian and Eritrean support was crucial in placing the principle of self-determination on the negotiating table of the IGAD talks. When the US became involved in the peace process in 2002 the president's special envoy on Sudan, Senator Danforth, famously declared that independence for the South would be "a bad idea".

Now, let's look at the tally. When the war began in 1983 Khartoum had the support of the US and Egypt, and the SPLA had the support of Ethiopia and Libya. Israel had been neutralized by the Camp David Agreement, Uganda was preoccupied with its own internal troubles, and China was only one of Sudan's trading partners. At the end of the war in 2005 Khartoum had the support of Egypt and Libya and had picked up China along the way (and to a certain extent India and Malaysia as well). The SPLA had the support of the US, Ethiopia and Uganda. Those American political and religious groups who had supported Khartoum at the start of the war now proclaimed themselves fervent supporters of South Sudanese independence all along. The fallout of the Ethiopian-Eritrean war left Eritrea on the sidelines seeking whatever alignment might hurt Ethiopia most. Kenya and Norway, though more neutral than most, were at least friendly to the new government in Juba.

So, few permanent friends here, and alliances that shifted according to how the interests were best served. What implications does this have for South Sudan's future as an independent nation?

The South's experiences during the last two wars demonstrate that in international relations there is no such thing as a permanent friend, even if governments will proclaim a rhetorical permanence out of diplomatic nicety. National interests can dictate an alternation between friendliness and hostility. Friends today can be enemies tomorrow, and vice versa. As South Sudan's own civil war, beginning in 2013, has demonstrated even friends can be dangerous. These are lessons that no government can afford to forget. South Sudan, too, will have to define its own *national* interests and decide on the best way to pursue them. It will be in its interests to be on good terms with *all* its neighbours. If they cannot be good *friends*, they can at least have good *relations*. Looking beyond that immediate circle South Sudan will need to cultivate good relations with those countries who have interests in the South, but to do so it will need to understand what those interests really are, always recognising that the majority of nations will be neither friends nor enemies.

PEOPLE

13
LANGUAGES OF SOUTH SUDAN

There are more languages spoken in Africa than on any other continent. This is not surprising given that Africa was the cradle of humankind, and humans have been living in Africa longer than on any other continent. Within Africa Sudan contained one of the highest numbers of living languages, one hundred thirty-three at one recent count. And of those one hundred thirty-three over half are spoken in South Sudan.

One of the problems of counting languages, of course, is that distinctions must be made between separate languages and dialects of the same language. And here linguists often disagree and keep changing their minds. Linguists also look for connections between languages in fundamental structure and vocabulary, grouping them into language families. This is also where they disagree and classifications keep changing as more detailed linguistic research is done, altering theories about language families and groups.

Take for instance two classifications proposed in the nineteenth century, based on a Biblical understanding of the ancient world. The names of two language families – "Semitic" and "Hamitic" – were derived from two of Noah's sons: Shem and Ham. "Semitic" continues as a name for the related languages of Arabic, Hebrew and Amharic, but the use of "Hamitic" is more problematic. It was more about early race theories than language.

In late-nineteenth and early-twentieth century ethnology the "Hamites" were thought to be a race of near-European origin who brought statecraft and other benefits of "higher civilization" to sub-Saharan Africa. Wherever a state existed, from highland Ethiopia to the Great Lakes to Great Zimbabwe, there, it was said, the Hamites had been. Certain physical features, such as lighter skin and thin noses, were thought to be evidence of the

Hamitic presence; thus the creation of "Nilo-Hamites", the offspring of Hamitic unions with black Africans.

The twentieth-century study of Africa revised this race theory. There is no genetic, linguistic, or archaeological evidence to support the idea of the existence of a Hamitic race. What became known as the "Hamitic Hypothesis" in African history has been replaced by more subtle and diverse theories about population migrations, the spread of language, culture, state-building and so on. Belief in the existence of the Hamitic race is now confined to those who accept chapter 10 of the book of Genesis as literal and historic truth.

The Hamites might have been discarded by mainstream academics, but Nilo-Hamites clung on, especially in writings about Sudan, mainly through the lingering influence of C.G. Seligman's *The Pagan Tribes of the Nilotic Sudan* and his much re-edited *The Races of Africa* (now, thankfully, out of print). Even after the racial theories from which the term sprang were widely repudiated "Nilo-Hamitic" continued as a linguistic classification until Joseph Greenberg produced a new classification of Africa's languages in the 1960s. Greenberg's identification of language families and language groups in Africa has become the basis for most subsequent linguistic research, though the names and composition of these families and groups continue to be debated. But two of Greenberg's conclusions are now widely accepted: there are no such language families as "Hamitic" or "Nilo-Hamitic".

Despite this linguistic consensus of the last fifty years, "Nilo-Hamites" keep on popping up in writing about Sudan and especially South Sudan. So, let us be absolutely clear about this. If there is no such thing as "Hamites", there can be no such thing as "Nilo-Hamites", their supposed offspring. There are no "Hamitic" languages, and there are no "Nilo-Hamitic" languages.

Where does this leave the peoples and languages of South Sudan, and why does it matter? It matters because linguistically most peoples of South Sudan are not isolated from each other or from the rest of Africa. They belong to the same broad language family, now generally called Nilo-Saharan, and this family not only includes most of the languages of South Sudan, but many of East Africa, Ethiopia, northern Sudan, and the Saharan-Sahelian belt of Africa.

The Nilo-Saharan family includes languages spoken by peoples within Sudan as far apart as the Nubians in the north, the Fur, Zaghawa and Berti in Darfur, the Gumuz, Ingessana (Gaamk), Uduk and Komo of Blue Nile. Beyond Sudan the Nilo-Saharan family includes Kunama in Eritrea, Berta in Ethiopia, Kanuri in Chad, Mangbetu and Lendu in Congo, Lugbara and Lango in Uganda, and Maasai and Kalenjin in Kenya.

Who in South Sudan is part of the Nilo-Saharan family? There are several divisions within the family. The Central Sudanic division includes Moru, Madi, Avokaya and Lugbara from the Ugandan border region (East Central branch), and Bongo, Baka, Beli, Jur Modo, Mittu, Yulu, Kresh, Aja, Gbaya of Western Bahr el-Ghazal (West Central branch). The Central Sudanic division also includes Lendu and Mangbetu of Congo and Bagirmi of Chad. The Eastern Sudanic division includes Njangulgule of Western Bahr el-Ghazal, Didinga and Narim of Eastern Equatoria, and Suri (or Kichepo) and Murle of Jonglei. Beyond South Sudan it also includes Nubian, Fur, Daju, Shatt, Ingessana and Mursi.

Perhaps the best known branch of Eastern Sudanic, and the one that includes most of the Nilo-Saharan speakers in South Sudan, is the Nilotic division. Western Nilotic includes Nuer, Dinka, Shilluk, Anyuak and Mabaan of greater Upper Nile, but also Luo and Belanda Bor of greater Bahr el-Ghazal and Pari and Acholi of greater Equatoria. These languages are closely related to Luo of Kenya. Eastern Nilotic (some of whom used to be classed as "Nilo-Hamites") are found mainly in greater Equatoria: Bari, Pöjulu, Kakwa, Kuku, and Mundari of Central Equatoria; Toposa, Jiye, and Nyangatom of Eastern Equatoria, and Lotuho and Lokoya. Toposa, Jiye and Nyangatom are sometimes called part of the "Ateker Cluster", which also includes Karimojong and Turkana of Uganda and Kenya, while the Lotuho and Lokoya languages are related to Maasai in Kenya and Tanzania.

While the Nilo-Saharan languages are the most numerous of the vernacular languages of South Sudan, there is a separate language family found in the south-west part of the country. Zande belongs to the Niger-Congo family that stretches from West Africa through Central and East Africa and on down to southern Africa, the most numerous examples being the Bantu branch of the Niger-Congo family. Zande is a very distant cousin to Bantu.

The above classifications are used to identify historically related languages, and the names used to classify them are to a certain extent arbitrary. Gone are the days of applying racial categories (mythical or real) to languages, and these days the names applied are broadly geographical (Nilo-Saharan, Niger-Congo, Sudanic), vaguely historical (Cushitic, Songhay), or derived from shared common words (such as "Bantu"). But whereas linguists have tried to apply neutral-sounding names, these names are sometimes resisted.

In South Sudan, as in Uganda, some of the regional political divisions have been described in broadly ethnic terms, as in Equatorians vs. "Nilotics" (South Sudan) or Bantu of the south vs. "Nilotics" of the north (Uganda). The word "Nilotic" does not cover the same language groups in each country. Whereas "Nilotic" in South Sudan is generally understood to mean the Western Nilotic-speaking Dinka and Nuer, it is not colloquially applied in this way to the Western Nilotic-speaking Acholi or Pari of Equatoria. And while in Uganda the so-called "Nilotics" do include the Acholi and Lango of the north, they also include such non-Western Nilotic peoples as the Lugbara of West Nile. And let's not even mention Ethiopia, where "Nilotic" is applied to anyone in the southern lowlands, irrespective of their native language.

"Nilotic", therefore, can be a confusing, even an emotional term. I remember in the 1970s some Equatorian students who were introduced to African linguistics for the first time in the University of Khartoum were offended to be told that they were "Eastern Nilotic". They vehemently denied that they were "Nilotic". In the early 1980s one Equatorian I knew insisted that Equatorians were "Bantu" in opposition to "Nilotics", a usage that he had picked up in exile in Uganda.

All countries have their internal political differences, and these differences are often read back into history. But the study of history is the search for real connections, for real origins, and it can be a way to expand beyond parochial concerns. On the 9th of July 2011 in Juba I sat next to two African guests at South Sudan's independence celebrations. One was a Karimojong from Uganda, the other was a Luo from Kenya. We discussed similarities between their languages and some of the languages of South Sudan. For them South Sudan's independence marked a reconnection with the rest of Africa, a final placing of a strategic piece in the jigsaw puzzle of the African past. "This is our home," one of them said to me. "This is where we came from." The study of the languages of Africa shows that South Sudan is truly connected to the rest of Africa: north, south, east and west.

Further reading:
    Joseph, Greenberg, *The Languages of Africa*
    Christopher Ehret, *The Civilizations of Africa: a history to 1800*

14
ARE SOUTH SUDANESE ANIMISTS?

Sudan is divided between the Muslim North and the Christian and Animist South. We know this because nearly every news story about the North-South political divide tells us so. Whatever a correspondent might write from the field, a sub-editor back in the office will tack on that line. You will see it in Reuters reports out of Cairo, Khartoum and Juba; you will find it posted on Sudan Tribune; it jumps out at you from *The Economist* and *Time;* it ambushes you in *The Times,* the *Guardian,* the *Daily Telegraph,* the *New York Times,* the *Washington Post,* and every metropolitan and provincial newspaper that cares to mention Sudan from Adelaide, Australia to Zapata, Texas. We know it must be true, otherwise all the world's media would be wrong.

But just what is an "animist", and are there any in Sudan?

"Animism" has no single meaning. Or, rather, it has at least two. Its first meaning was defined by the man who invented the word, the British anthropologist, E.B. Tylor (1832-1917). For Tylor "animism" did not apply to any single type of religion; rather, it described a theory about the origin of religion. He speculated that religion arose when "primitive men" (by which he meant humanity's pre-historic ancestors) tried to explain how they were able to meet and speak with dead people in their dreams. Tylor assumed that "primitive man" would believe that dreams were real, and therefore they believed they really did speak with their dead ancestors, relatives or friends when they dreamed about them. It is on these dreams, Tylor asserted, that the belief in ghosts and the existence of the immaterial soul was first based, and out of that came the belief in the afterlife, and from that came the belief in spirits and the supernatural world.

According to Tylor "Spirits are simply personified causes. As men's ordinary life and actions were held to be caused by souls, so the happy or disastrous events which affect mankind, as well as the manifold physical operations of the outer-world, were accounted for as caused by soul-like beings", in other words "spirits". From this developed the idea of ancestor cults (ghosts where turned into benevolent deities), or that animals might have souls, and that spirits might reside in specific objects, such as trees or stones (fetishes).

The trouble with this theory, as most anthropologists, philosophers and theologians will tell us today, is that it is impossible to prove. It is an evolutionary argument for the existence of religion, which ranks religions along a scale from inferior to superior and implicitly places some (mainly the monotheistic religions) at a higher level of development than others (for example, all African religions).

But quite apart from being unable to prove that this is how our pre-historic ancestors thought, there is the lack of evidence that the people who practice so-called primitive religions today also think this way. The 20th century British anthropologist, Evans-Pritchard, who wrote about many of South Sudan's people, including the Azande, Nuer, and Anyuak, observed "it remains to be proved that the most primitive peoples think that creatures and material objects have souls like their own. If any peoples can be said to be dominantly animistic, in Tylor's sense of the word, they belong to much more advanced cultures, a fact which, though it would have no historical significance for me, would be highly damaging to the evolutionary argument."

So, there are two basic meanings of the word "animism": 1) a theory that religion first emerged as an explanation for dreams about the dead, and 2) a belief that the natural world is animated by souls or spirits inside natural objects, whether stones, plants or animals. Anyone who subscribes to Tylor's theory about the origin of religion, therefore, is an animist of the first definition, and I doubt that there are any animists of that type in South Sudan today. What of the second type?

Turning to the anthropologists again, not a single one who has made a serious study of the religious beliefs and practices of the many different South Sudanese societies has described them as "animist". Quite the contrary. They have even resisted describing them as polytheistic. Take Evans-Pritchard again. He noted that the Nuer use their word for "God" or "Spirit" both in the singular (*Kuoth*) and in the plural (*kuuth*). There are many different names for the different *kuuth*: Deng, Diu, Wiu, Teny, Maani (or Maadni), Gar, Cak, etc. These *kuuth* often seize a person, who then speaks with their voice, becoming a *guk kuoth* – "Container of Spirit" – or a prophet. Yet while Nuer acknowledge these various named *kuuth*, they also claim that they are all one – they are all aspects of *Kuoth* speaking in different voices to different communities, not separate, competing, conflicting divinities. One old man confirmed this to me many years ago when I was asking him about these *kuuth*. "They are all the same", he said finally, putting an end to my litany of names.

The Dinka are very similar to the Nuer. When a Nuer or Dinka prays to a named divinity, they do so rather as Catholics pray to saints, seeking their intercession with God, but not treating them as independent spirits or divinities separate from God. While not all South Sudanese religions are like the Nuer or Dinka, none, as far as I know, can truly be described as "animistic". Yet despite Evans-Pritchard's description, and his explicit statement that the Nuer are *not* animists, still you find them described as "praying to their animist gods" (as a correspondent in *Time* once wrote). So how did this word get started?

The problem started with the missionaries. They had a ready terminology for the people they intended to convert, having brought with them the word "pagan" from the days when they were battling for souls with the old temple religions of the Roman Empire. They found pagans galore in the southern Sudan when they first arrived in the nineteenth century. But "pagan" is redolent of Christian propaganda, and in the 1950s and 1960s, as the Sudan and other African countries became independent, missionaries became increasingly uncomfortable with using such a prejudicial term. There was also a strong dialogue between missionary and anthropological studies of African religions, and while British Social Anthropologists in Sudan and East Africa had rejected the term "animism", it appeared to have a more neutral and scientific value than "paganism". In fact, French anthropologists working in West Africa popularised the term as scientific. So, yesterday's pagans became today's animists.

Interestingly enough I have met one self-confessed animist in South Sudan. He was a Japanese anthropologist. Japanese religion, he explained to me, is animistic, in the second sense of the word, so he was an animist. As more Japanese come to South Sudan to work or study, so the community of animists will grow from one to...more than one?

Some South Sudanese, aware of the prevalence of the term but unaware of its meaning, have adopted it and applied it to themselves. I have seen South Sudanese refer to "we Christians and animists", and even to "we Christian animists", an interesting conflation of two opposed ideas. Perhaps South Sudanese readers should clarify this point. Does any reader believe that stones, plants and animals are animated by spirits? Is this a personal belief, or one shared more widely in the community? Details would be appreciated.

Further reading:
    E. E. Evans-Pritchard, *Nuer Religion*
    E. E. Evans-Pritchard, *Theories of Primitive Religion*
    R. G. Lienhardt, *Divinity and Experience: the religion of the Dinka*

15
WHAT DID NGUNDENG REALLY SAY AND DO?

The report that South Sudanese church leaders intended to travel to Israel to fulfill an alleged Old Testament prophecy by Isaiah sparked off yet another religious debate on the internet. It is not so much a debate about Isaiah and the Bible as about one of South Sudan's own prophets, the nineteenth century Lou Nuer, Ngundeng Bong. What Ngundeng said, or did not say, has become an emotional topic because of the way he was invoked by some of the actors in the fighting in Jonglei State during the 1990s and in South Sudan's own civil war. The internet debate is mainly between members of South Sudan's diaspora, and it is clear that neither those correspondents who denounce Ngundeng as Satan, nor those who revere him as a divine prophet are writing with any clear knowledge of what he is supposed to have done or said.

There are a number of ways to approach Ngundeng (or any other historical religious figure, for that mater). You can approach him as a historian, trying to find out what he said, did, and meant to the people of his own time. You can approach him as a believer, where what he meant in his own time is less important than what he means to you today. Or you can approach him as many evangelists do, dismissing him (and all other traditional religious figures) as evil Satanists to be swept aside by a more militant Christianity or Islam. As I am neither a believer nor an evangelist it is probably unwise for an historian (and a foreigner) to intervene in a religious debate; nevertheless there is some value in trying to establish what we can know about this important historical figure.

The Nuer move with their cattle, and in the nineteenth century this meant that they moved into a vast territory both north and south of the Sobat river. The Nuer have the reputation of being fierce fighters, but they also have the reputation for assimilation, and Nuer society underwent profound changes in the nineteenth century as a result of their contact with and absorption of the peoples in what is now Jonglei State. The old cohesion was strained both by movement and the incorporation of new persons with kin-ties extending beyond Nuer society. Feuds were more difficult to resolve if one group could just move off to occupy new territory. Attacking old enemies like the Dinka or Anyuak could cause problems closer to home if people in one section now also had close relatives among those being attacked by another section.

Ngundeng claimed to speak with the voice of Deng – a divine figure known to both Nuer and Dinka as well as to many peoples throughout the upper Nile basin. As a prophet of Deng he addressed many issues affecting the social cohesion of Nuer society and Nuer relations with their neighbours. He opposed the use of private magic for personal gain, so much so that he banished his eldest son for dabbling in it. He condemned both inter-sectional feuds among the Nuer and cattle raids against the Dinka – something that the British, no friends of Ngundeng, later confirmed.

But the paradox of Ngundeng as a prophet of peace was that he secured his reputation through victory in a major battle. In about 1879 the Lou Nuer were attacked by a coalition of Dinka and Gaawar Nuer, led by an ex-soldier from the Egytian army (he was described as being circumcised and carrying a sword or bayonet), but Ngundeng decisively defeated them at Pading, near Khor Fulluth (Nuer for "the Pool of the Lungfish"). Some of the earliest recorded eye-witness accounts of this battle indicate that Ngundeng laid an ambush for the invading force and pushed them back into the swampy area where they were defeated. Later versions, however, attribute his victory entirely to his spiritual power. In these versions Ngundeng killed his attackers through the power of his decorated stick – the *dang* (rod or baton). He raised it to the sky, invoked his divinity, and his enemies died.

The problem with gaining an early reputation for military victory is that people expect you to repeat it. When a British-led armed column approached Ngundeng's village in 1902 the Lou expected him to repeat his victory at Pading. Ngundeng raised his *dang*, announced that his divinity was not present, and disbanded his force. Whether Ngundeng acted through divine inspiration, or he made a shrewd assessment of the chances of the spear-armed Nuer against the rifle-armed soldiers of the Anglo-Egyptian army, we will never know for sure. The soldiers demonstrated their pacific intentions by burning Ngundeng's village and confiscating the ivory tusks surrounding his shrine.

By refusing to fight Ngundeng avoided the fate that finally befell his son Guek Ngundeng in 1929. When the government of the day accused Guek of plotting a rebellion he at first tried to evade the army but was rebuked by his age-mates, who claimed that if Ngundeng were alive he would have defeated the army just as he had defeated his foes at Pading. When Guek finally confronted the Sudan Defence Force in front of his father's shrine and tried to re-enact his father's famous victory he was shot dead along with a number of his followers, and his body was hung from a tree for all to see his fate.

This is a bare outline of what can be determined through a combination of Nuer eye-witness testimony and contemporary British documents. I published a more comprehensive account nearly twenty years ago in a book entitled *Nuer Prophets*. But the eye-witnesses are now all dead, the documents inaccessible in foreign archives, and the book too expensive for most South Sudanese to afford. In these circumstances it's not surprising that alternative versions of Ngundeng's life are circulating among believers. In these versions Ngundeng's victory at Pading is conflated with his encounter with the Anglo-Egyptian army near his shrine. Far from dispersing his own force Ngundeng is now said to have defeated the British through the use of his *dang*. Even Guek is credited with shooting down one of the Royal Air Force's airplanes. This, interestingly enough, is almost true. The government deployed four bi-planes against the Lou when they were chasing Guek. These were wood and fabric constructions that did not offer their pilots much protection. One pilot was hit in the thigh by a shot from below by a Nuer rifleman. He did not crash, but while he recovered from his wound back at base there was no one to fly his airplane, and the RAF squadron was reduced from four to three.

The attempt to re-enact prophecy can be dangerous and cost Guek his life. Trying to anticipate the fulfillment of prophecy might not always be so dangerous, but it is, shall we say, just as unpredictable. At the time of Guek a prophecy attributed to his father circulated concerning the road the British wanted the Nuer to build by hand. The road would stop at a place called "noor bor" and "things would be finished" – the government would go away. That didn't happen. Some fifty years later this prophecy was revived, only now it was applied to the building of the Jonglei canal. The canal was halted and remains unfinished today, and "noor bor" was taken to mean the 1983 Bor mutiny and the founding of the SPLA. You would expect that such a convincing concurrence of events would establish the final interpretation, but not so. Some now say "noor bor" refers to the 1991 attack on Bor by the Nasir faction and Lou Nuer White Army.

Perhaps the most persistent prophecy, and the one so constantly re-interpreted, is the one about the "Turuk col", the "Black Turks". This, too, became current during the time of Guek, when it was said that Ngundeng foretold a time when the Nuer would be turned into "Black Turks" (the Nuer word for the Anglo-Egyptian invaders and anyone associated with government) before becoming free. In the 1920s this was taken to mean the chiefs' police, Nuer recruited into the service of the newly created Native Administration. In the 1970s the "Black Turks" prophecy was applied to the formation of the Southern

Regional Government. Today it is applied to the government of the independent Republic of South Sudan.

Let us not even try to identify the figure in Ngundeng's prophecy that peace would be brought by a left-handed man. Ngundeng was left-handed, and all mention of a left-handed man in his songs refer to himself, but over the years there have been many attempts to identify other left-handed peace makers. Abel Alier, whose successful negotiation of the Addis Ababa Agreement ended the first civil war, is left-handed. US President George W. Bush is left-handed, and many South Sudanese give him credit for re-starting the IGAD negotiations that led to the CPA. There have been many recent embellishments to make the prophecy fit other candidates. I recorded over three hundred Ngundeng songs in the 1970s and none of them included the names or descriptions that have been circulating in favour of other claimants. What is clear is that if peace is to return to South Sudan, it will take more than one man, and both hands, to bring it.

Further reading:
Douglas H. Johnson, *Nuer Prophets: history and prophecy from the Upper Nile*
Douglas H. Johnson, "The prophet Ngundeng and the battle of Pading: prophecy, symbolism and historical evidence", in David M. Anderson and Douglas H. Johnson (eds), *Revealing Prophets: prophecy in Eastern African history*

16
IS THIS NGUNDENG'S PHOTOGRAPH?

There is a photograph of a Nuer prophet (now over a hundred years old) that has appeared on various South Sudanese websites. Many claim that it is a contemporary picture of the prophet Ngundeng Bong; some aren't so sure. I'm not surprised that this photo has surfaced at this time, now that Ngundeng is being presented by many as a prophet of the South Sudanese nation. The need for heroes in South Sudan is strong, and the heroes of the past need some physical, immediately identifiable, representation. I'm also not surprised that many identify this photo with Ngundeng. Years ago I used to show this photo to the Lou whom I interviewed about the prophets, and they almost all identified it as Ngundeng.

Figure 2: Major Gwynn's Photo of a Nuer Prophet, c. 1900-03
(Source: Pitt Rivers Museum, Oxford)

But is it? If the photo really is that of Ngundeng then some British officer or government official must have met him. So, what is the evidence for that?

Contemporary government records present Ngundeng as an elusive figure. In 1902 the governor of Upper Nile Province marched with a column of soldiers to Ngundeng's village of Weideang. He sent a threatening message to Ngundeng to come to him and "submit". When he received no reply, he burned the village and looted the ivory tusks that surround Ngundeng's Mound (*biɛ*). We have a number of photographs of the Mound (the misnamed "pyramid") taken at that time, but of Ngundeng, none. On other occasions when British officials marched along the borders of Lou Nuer territory Ngundeng was reported to have moved further away to avoid contact. His antipathy to things of the *hakuma* (government) was such that a Dinka refugee from Cairo visiting friends and family on the Khor Fulluth in 1904 reported that Ngundeng not only refused to talk to him, but covered his face to avoid looking at his clothes. The nearest any government official got to Ngundeng was in 1906 when the deputy governor of Upper Nile again tried to contact him, but by the time he reached Weideang Ngundeng had died, and the Lou would not even show him where Ngundeng was buried.

The British record, therefore, is clear. No British officer or government official ever met Ngundeng, or even saw him in the distance. And this, too, is confirmed by what Ngundeng's family told me forty years ago. Ngundeng never met the *hakuma*.

So, who took this photo, where was it taken, who is pictured, and how did we get to know about it?

The photograph was taken by Major Charles Gwynn of the Royal Engineers, who in 1900 and 1903 was surveying Sudan's border with Ethiopia. In 1900 he travelled from Gidami south to Nasir and then along the Sobat to Fashoda. He returned in 1903, this time coming in the opposite direction, from Fashoda to Nasir and then on to Itang. From Itang he was accompanied by an Ethiopian official to Khor Machar, where he placed a boundary marker, and from Khor Machar they went to the junction of the Sobat and Pibor rivers, then up river as far as the Gaajok village of Koratong. This is all documented in Gwynn's contemporary reports.

The photograph, then, was taken either in 1900 or 1903, while Ngundeng was alive. It was not taken in a Lou Nuer village, but in either in a Gaajak or Gaajok village, where Ngundeng had influence. In the Gaajak area, especially, Ngundeng had a number of disciples, minor prophets who, like Ngundeng, claimed to be possessed by divinity, sang Ngundeng's songs, and imitated Ngundeng's appearance. The man in the photo is what government officials of the day called a *kujur*, a colloquial Arabic term applied to many different types of spiritual figures whether a prophet (*guk*), prophet's disciple (*dayiem*), or magician (*guan wal*). My guess is that this was one of Ngundeng's Gaajak *dayiemni*. We won't know for sure, unless Gwynn's private papers relating to the survey are found and the time and place of the photograph can be identified with greater certainty.

Years after the photo was taken Gwynn lent the photo to the British anthropologist, Evans-Pritchard, for use in his book, *Nuer Religion*, published in 1956. When Evans-Pritchard worked among the Nuer in the 1930s all the major prophets had just been suppressed by the government: Guek Ngundeng was dead, Dual Diu, Car Koryom and Pok Kerjiok were all in prison. Evans-Pritchard heard a lot about Ngundeng and these other prophets, but he never met them. But prophets usually had a distinctive appearance, letting their hair and beards grow, unlike other Nuer men, and he used this photo of an unnamed minor prophet to illustrate the distinctive appearance of prophets among the Nuer, and to contrast that with the appearance of the "priest" – the *kuar muon* or leopard-skin chief.

The original print of the photo is now in the Pitt-Rivers Museum in Oxford, as part of their extensive collection of photographs and material culture from South Sudan. The photograph can be found on their website. It is most likely from this source that copies of the photo now seen on other websites was taken.

When I took a copy of *Nuer Religion* with me to show to Lou Nuer, and they asserted that the photo was of Ngundeng, I would ask how did they know? Almost always they said that it was because Ngundeng was left-handed, and the man in the photo was left handed. Except that he is not. He has his back to the camera and the spear he is holding aloft is clearly in his right hand. Final proof – if by now it were needed – that the man in the picture is not Ngundeng. But for someone who is not used to looking at photographic images (as my Lou informants were not), they might have assumed the figure was facing the camera, and therefore the spear was held in the left hand.

We have no contemporary image of Jesus Christ. There is a debate about what he looked like: did he have long hair or short, did he have a beard or was he clean-shaven? Many early Greek depictions show him with short hair and clean-shaven in the contemporary Hellenic style. But because of centuries of religious art we now think we know what Jesus looked like, and his features are immediately recognizable to any familiar with that art. To those who need to know what Ngundeng looked like, this photo is the nearest approximation they can get. The figure was a contemporary of Ngundeng's, and he may have been a disciple who consciously imitated Ngundeng's appearance. I suspect that arguments about the historical authenticity of this photograph will carry little weight with those who need to believe. As South Sudan develops its own artistic forms – both religious and nationalistic – let us see what image of Ngundeng emerges.

Further reading:
 E. E. Evans-Pritchard, *Nuer Religion*

17
SOUTH SUDANESE MISSIONARIES: CATERINA ZEINAB, TRANSLATOR AND EVANGELIST

In 2000 Sudanese Christians got their first saint, Josephine Bakhita, the ex-slave from Darfur, after whom Radio Bakhita is named. But while Bakhita converted to Christianity and joined an order of nuns in Italy, she never returned to Sudan and never ministered to Sudanese Christians. One woman who did was Bakhita's contemporary, Caterina Zeinab (c.1848-1921). Caterina is one of several early South Sudanese Christians, such as Daniel Surur Farim Deng (c.1865-1900) and Salim Charles Wilson (c.1860-1946) (chapters 18 & 19), who until recently, have been largely overlooked in histories of Sudanese Christianity.

Caterina Zeinab was born around 1848 in the Cic Dinka village of Gog, near the Bahr el-Jebel. We don't know her Dinka name, but the name of her father has come down to us as Manyan e Agol. In 1854 the Catholic Fathers from Verona (both Italian and Austrian) founded their first station in the southern Sudan near Caterina's village at a location variously called Santa Croce, Heiliges Kreuz, Holy Cross, or just Kanisa ("church" in Arabic). The missionaries reported that they found the Dinka receptive to their message, in part because they felt that the mission offered them some protection from the nearby trading stations of the ivory and slave merchants. But there was a high mortality rate among the missionaries, and in 1860 the station was closed. When the missionaries returned to Khartoum they brought with them a small number of Dinka children, among them the girl then named Zeinab.

We don't have any autobiographical account that explains why Zeinab chose (or was chosen) to go with the missionaries, or why she converted to Christianity. We do know that she was baptised as "Caterina" at the Catholic church in Shellal, Egypt in 1860, and by her subsequent education and activities became the first Dinka Christian evangelist. She turned out to be a skilled linguist in Dinka, Arabic and Italian. While being educated in Egypt she helped the missionaries compile a Dinka dictionary and grammar and translate the first Dinka Catholic catechism. She was sent for further education to Verona in 1862, where she was confirmed. In 1867 she returned to Cairo to teach in the mission schools there, and she also served as a catechist among resident Dinka. She finally returned to Khartoum in 1873, teaching in the mission school and assisting in baptisms, and earned the reputation as "a very talented missionary".

Caterina never took holy orders, but instead married an Italian carpenter, Cesare Ongano, in 1874. He died in 1875, only a few months after the birth of their daughter, Emilia. Caterina returned to the mission, but Emilia died in 1878. We don't know how these losses affected her, but shortly thereafter she left the mission and began living with Ernst Marno, an Austrian explorer then employed by Egypt as the governor of the border province of Fazoghli. They never married, but in 1880 Caterina gave birth to a son, Jacob Ernst in Fashoda, who was subsequently baptised in Khartoum in 1881.

This was the beginning of hard times for Caterina. Marno died in Khartoum in 1883. She remained in that city throughout the subsequent siege of 1884-5. For unexplained reasons General Gordon, the governor-general during the siege, disliked Caterina – but then he doesn't seem to have liked any African women. Caterina and her son were in Khartoum when it fell to the Mahdi's army, but they both survived. For the next thirteen years they lived in Omdurman with other Christian residents: Greek and European merchants and their families, the few remaining Catholic priests and nuns. Not quite prisoners, and not quite hostages, these Christians were unable to leave Omdurman except in a few dramatic escapes, such as those of Fathers Rossignoli and Ohrwalder. Outwardly these Christians had to adopt Mahdist dress, and the Catholic church suspected them of apostasy. But many of them continued to meet and worship in secret, and Caterina might have been among their number.

The defeat of the Mahdist forces at the battle of Omdurman in 1898 and the establishment of the Anglo-Egyptian condominium over Sudan allowed the Christians to once again worship openly. Caterina went to Cairo shortly after the fall of Omdurman but returned to Khartoum in 1902 and resumed work with the church there, acting as an interpreter. The Church planned to employ her in a new mission among the Shilluk (where her son Jacob had been born), but she declined on the grounds of ill health, did no more active mission work, and lived on an Egyptian government pension as Marno's widow until her death in Khartoum in 1921. Jacob lived on, working as a ghaffir for the Comboni mission and died in 1955.

The Church prefers to remember and honour those faithful who take orders and so dedicate their lives to God. There is a distinct hint of disappointment in Caterina Zeinab in the Catholic church's post-reconquest reports. The once "very talented missionary" had lost a husband and lost a child, then had an unsanctified union with another man and a child out of wedlock. After brief re-employment by the Church she then declined to do any further mission work. This is not the makings of a saint like Josephine Bakhita, who ended her life in an Italian nunnery, far away from her own people. But of the two Caterina had a greater impact on the spread of Christianity in Sudan in her own life-time, having spent almost all of her life in Sudan and Egypt in direct contact with other Sudanese. Through her translation work in the mid-nineteenth century she helped the Church lay the foundation for later missionary proselytizing. Through her teaching in Cairo and Khartoum she introduced other Sudanese to Church doctrine. As an interpreter in the early twentieth century she mediated between newly returned churchmen and the different Sudanese communities of Khartoum.

With her fluency in both Dinka and Arabic Caterina taught displaced Sudanese in Cairo and Khartoum, a mixed population that included many slaves and was noted for assimilating a wide variety of spiritual practices and beliefs. Under Anglo-Egyptian rule many of these displaced persons returned to their homes in South Sudan. In the late-twentieth century writers such as Francis Deng recorded very Christian-sounding stories from modern Dinka who claimed these were tales learned from their grand-parents. It doesn't require too much of a stretch of the imagination to suggest that the train of transmission might stretch back to Caterina. We will never know for sure, but the fact that Caterina's influence is largely undocumented does not mean that she had no influence at all.

Caterina Zeinab's life reminds us that history is not made just by great men and women, but also by ordinary persons who live in extraordinary times. In many ways, too, Caterina was extraordinary: she would have been only about twelve years old when she left her home and her family, never to see them again, to embark on a new life in strange lands, speaking new languages, but returning to her country with new skills and education. In that respect the pattern of her life has been repeated by many South Sudanese today: displaced by war, who grew up abroad as refugees, but who obtained the education they could not get at home. Caterina is unlikely ever to be sanctified by the church she served, nor will she ever be recognized as the patron saint of the displaced, but she can be honoured by those who have shared a similar life experience and now have returned home with the skills needed to rebuild their country.

Further reading:
    Douglas H. Johnson, "Divinity abroad: Dinka missionaries in foreign lands", in Wendy James & Douglas H. Johnson (eds), *Vernacular Christianity: essays on the social anthropology of religion presented to Godfrey Lienhardt*
    Douglas H. Johnson, "Zenab, Caterina", *Dictionary of African Biography*

18
SOUTH SUDANESE MISSIONARIES: FR. DANIEL SURUR FARIM DENG, SLAVE AND THEOLOGIAN

The Reverend Father Daniel Surur Farim Deng (c.1865-1900) was a former slave who became the first South Sudanese to be ordained a Christian priest. Like his near contemporary, Caterina Zeinab (c.1848-1921), his life was transformed by contact with the Italian priest Daniel Comboni (1831-1881). Like his other contemporary, Salim Charles Wilson (c.1860-1946), the path that led him to his new religion lay through his experiences as a slave.

Farim Deng was born in the mid-nineteenth century. Descended from a Nuer family adopted into the Mareng section of the Ngok Dinka, he grew up in a village on the banks of the river Kiir. Throughout his early life the Ngok were harassed by raiding parties of Baggara nomads – one such raid was repulsed the very day he was born. Both his father and older brother died of natural causes while he was still young, leaving him with family responsibilities normally shouldered by older men.

In about 1871 a raiding party of Homr-Misseriya attacked the Mareng and Diil sections of the Ngok and Farim was captured along with his mother and sisters. The Dinka villages were put to the torch, the raiding party headed north, marching their captives and captured livestock across the savannah, raiding other settlements on the way, until they reached El Obeid, the capital of Kordofan Province. Farim was given the Arabic name of Surur, meaning joy or consolation. He and his mother were owned by the same man but were separated, his mother working in the owner's plantation outside El Obeid, and Farim herding his sheep. Throughout this time Farim did many jobs for his owner: herding sheep, selling milk and wild herbs in the market, working as a doorman, shopkeeper and tailor.

Years later he would write, "The state of a slave is like a living statue, from which the owner reaps as much profit as possible without worrying about what harms it. At that point a man knows and feels what losing his freedom means." His owner's overseer beat him, and one day, to escape another beating, he fled into the surrounding desert. There he faced a dilemma, whether to stay in the desert to die, or to seek shelter elsewhere. He knew of the mission in El Obeid where the Catholic Fathers from Verona ran a school for ex-slaves, but he had been told that the missionaries were slave-eating cannibals. Sitting under a tree outside town Farim considered what to do. At last, deciding that "death is no different if one is eaten by men or by wild beasts" he made his way to the mission, where he was interviewed by Monsignor Daniel Comboni himself. Comboni asked Farim who sent him, to which he replied, "God". Comboni laughed and took him in.

Daniel Comboni was one of the few priests to survive at the Santa Croce mission station on the Bahr el-Jebel where Caterina Zeinab lived. After his return to Italy in 1860 he decided that the future of missionary work in Africa lay with Africans, rather than Europeans. His "Plan for the Regeneration of Africa", as it became known, proposed "the regeneration of Africa by means of Africa itself". He returned to Sudan after 1872 and established a mission in El Obeid and another in the Nuba Mountains in order to recruit African converts for missionary training. Surur Farim Deng would become one of these recruits.

Farim's master first demanded the return of his slave, but Comboni refused. He then tried to buy him back, but that offer was also turned down. Finally he sent Farim's mother to try to coax him back with promises of better treatment, but Farim insisted on staying with the mission, later commenting about this decision, "A little firmness in certain decisive moments brings back the greatest victories and attracts singular graces from God." He never saw his mother or any other family members after that.

Farim began his religious education at the mission in El Obeid, being baptised in 1874 by Comboni who gave him the baptismal name of Daniel. So Farim now became Daniel Surur Farim Deng, each name commemorating a stage in his life from independence to servitude to liberation. In 1875 Comboni brought Daniel to Verona for further training, and in 1877 he was admitted to the Pontificio Collegio Urban di Propaganda Fide in Rome to train for the priesthood. After years of study in Rome, Beirut and Cairo Daniel Surur Farim Deng was ordained a Catholic priest in 1887, the first ever South Sudanese to join the priesthood.

As a student, and later as a teacher, Fr. Daniel was known for his competence in theology and his command of many languages: Italian, German, French, English along with Latin and Arabic, not to mention his native Dinka. His first posting after ordination was in the Red Sea port of Suakin, then the only Egyptian outpost left in Sudan and one frequently under siege from the Mahdist forces of the amir Osman Digna. He ministered to the small Christian community there for a couple of years, but because of his ability to preach in many languages he was sent on a European tour in 1889 to 1891 to raise money for the mission churches in Egypt and Suakin.

On his return to Egypt in 1891 he was based in the church at Heluan where his priestly duties included teaching children, visiting the sick and ministering to the poor. His congregation included Europeans, Egyptians and Sudanese. Never in robust health he had been sent to Europe in 1899 for rest but returned to Egypt an ill man. On 1 January 1900, though suffering from a high fever, he said Mass, as he later joked, "for all of 1900". It was his last Mass, as he died less than two weeks later. He lies buried in Cairo.

In missionary terms Fr. Daniel worked as a parish priest, and at the time of his death the Comboni ideal of "the regeneration of Africa by means of Africa itself" was far from being practiced in the Anglo-Egyptian Sudan. We can only speculate what impact he might have had in his homeland had he lived, and had either the church or the government allowed him to return. It was not until the 1940s, shortly before Sudanese independence, that the Catholic Church ordained any more South Sudanese priests. It was only after the expulsion of all foreign missionaries by an independent Sudanese government in the 1960s that the Sudanese churches became truly Sudanese. And it is only relatively recently that the Catholic Church granted Sudanese Christians their own saints: Josephine Bakhita in 2000 and Daniel Comboni in 2003. Of the two only Comboni, the European, ministered to Sudanese, both during his life in Sudan and after his death through the institutions he had founded. Perhaps in time they will also have a Saint Daniel Surur Farim Deng.

Further reading:
P.G.M.B., "Il Rev. P. Daniele Sorur. Nero della tribù dei Denka. Missionario dell'Africa Centrale", *Nigrizia*
Fr. Daniel Surur Farim Deng, "Memorie scritte dal R. P. Daniele Sorur Pharim Dèn", *Nigrizia*
Fr. Daniel Surur Farim Deng, "A Dinka priest writing on his own people", in Elias Toniolo and Richard Hill (eds), *The Opening of the Nile Basin*

19
SOUTH SUDANESE MISSIONARIES: SALIM WILSON THE "BLACK EVANGELIST OF THE NORTH"

We know a lot about European missionaries in Africa, and about European missionaries in South Sudan in particular. We know far less about African missionaries in Europe. There are, in fact, a growing number of clergy from African churches now active in places like Britain and the United States (Alaska's governor Sarah Palin was famously filmed with a Kenyan pastor praying for protection against witchcraft). But in the late nineteenth and early twentieth centuries there was a Sudanese missionary who spent his life preaching, not to the Sudanese, but to the English. He became known as Salim Charles Wilson, "The Black Evangelist of the North".

Figure 3: Salim Wilson at the Wilberforce Centennial, Hull
(Source: Salim Wilson, *I Was a Slave*)

Machar Kathiech, sometimes called "the Continuer" ("Hatashil" or "Athobhil"), was born around 1860 in the Gok Dinka village of Amerwai in what is now Pagoor Payam, Warrap state. He later described his father "Kathish" (or Kathiech) as a chief "by election". Some time around 1874 his village was attacked by slave-raiders, his father was killed in front of him, and Machar was taken as a slave. He was given the Arabic name Salim. His first master, whom he described as kind but poor, had to sell him to a brutal master, but Salim's chance for freedom came when Sulaiman Zubair, the son of Zubair Pasha and custodian of his trading empire in the Bahr al-Ghazal, rebelled against the Egyptian government. The Italian soldier of fortune, Romolo Gessi, was in charge of government troops who caught and executed Sulaiman in July 1879. It was shortly after this that Salim was freed by an Egyptian officer, who sent him back to Deim Zubair.

Salim might have ended up as any one of a number of young ex-slaves absorbed into the Egyptian army after Sulaiman's revolt. For a while he was attached to a Zande soldier who taught him how to trade and to hunt. But in November 1879 two British missionaries, C.T. Wilson and R.W. Felkin, arrived in Deim Zubair on their way home after being expelled from Buganda by the Kabaka Mutesa. Wilson needed a servant, and Salim pushed himself forward. Ten days later he left with his new employer on a journey that would take him away from his home and out of Sudan forever.

Arriving in England in 1880 Salim first went to the local village school in Pavenham, Bedfordshire, but later moved to Nottingham where he was baptised, keeping his Arabic name Salim, but taking on the name of his employer, Charles Wilson, as well. He was subsequently confirmed by the Bishop of Lincoln. He spent a short time at Hulme Cliff College, a missionary training institute, before leaving with the Wilsons for Palestine in 1883. It was in Palestine, at a hotel in Jaffa, that Salim met General Gordon for the first and only time (Gordon was on leave making a survey of the sacred places of the Holy Land). By this time Salim seems to have tired of the life of a servant and, borrowing ten pounds from his employer, returned to England and renewed his studies at Hulme Cliff.

By this time General Gordon had been sent to Sudan, had allowed himself to become besieged in Khartoum, and efforts at his rescue had become a hot political issue in Britain. The principal of Hulme Cliff took Salim on a tour of the north of England, dressed in a white turban, jallabiya and leopard skin, and exhibited him as a slave freed by General Gordon – a claim Salim had never made, and the credit for which should have gone to the nameless Egyptian officer.

After leaving college Salim did some work for the YMCA and the *British Women's Temperance Journal* in London, until he got his first chance at missionary work on an expedition to the Congo organized by a young English missionary with big ideas, Graham Wilmot Brooke. Brooke was a nineteenth-century advocate of what would now be called "the Clash of Cultures". The advance of Christianity in Africa, he claimed, was threatened by the twin advances of European commercial secularism and militant Islam, the most recent threat from the latter being the Jihad state of the Mahdi in Sudan. He proposed personally to confront the enemy in the borderlands between the Congo and Sudan, and for this he needed a companion who could speak Arabic. Salim, the former slave and Christian Dinka seemed heaven-sent. The expedition of the two missionaries started in Christian fellowship, but ended, inevitably, considering its unrealistic goal, in disappointment.

Salim and Brooke managed to get as far as the Ubangi River in north-eastern Congo where some disagreement between them ended the mission. Salim later wrote, "All this while Mr. Brooke had been gradually changing his theological views, and there came a sad day when we discovered that we could no longer see eye to eye in matters of doctrine, nor could we agree in our ideas as to what ought to be done when we found we could not get into the Soudan. So, eventually, there was nothing for it but that we should part company, which we did, with many regrets on my side."

The parting was probably due more to personal than theological differences. Brooke sought spiritual perfection away from secular contamination and he was often intolerant of African converts who sought self-improvement through education. Shortly after Brooke's death in Nigeria Salim wrote, "I felt at the time he was rather hard upon me, but if he erred, it was in judgment and not in heart."

Back in England Salim leant his services to the Church Missionary Society, who employed him for "missionary exhibition work", again often displayed wearing a leopard skin. He went on only one other mission to Africa when he accompanied two English missionaries to Tripoli in 1893 where he found he was able to converse with some Dinka slaves there. Shortly after the re-conquest of Sudan the British and Foreign Bible Society sought his advice on a translation of the Gospel of Luke into Dinka (based on an earlier translation made by a mid-nineteenth century German philologist). Salim's advice was frank, "I am afraid that Gospel in Dinka would be no use sending there, for the Dinka know nothing whatever of the art of reading. If you desirous to do good, the best is to establish schools at first, and certainly I would volunteer for that work. I have not much learning because I have no chance, but still natural experience of the people is something."

In the end the CMS were not interested in Salim's natural experience. In the racial hierarchy of the British Empire at the time African converts were subordinate to European missionaries, not their equals in Christ. Salim was to fulfil his missionary calling not in Africa, but in England, and more in non-conformist circles than in the established Anglican church. He obtained a lay reader's license from the Bishop of Wakefield in Yorkshire and for the next few decades he preached mainly in Lincolnshire and Yorkshire where he earned the title "the Black Evangelist of the North".

Shortly before World War I he moved to Scunthorpe in Lincolnshire and, in 1913, married his landlady, a widow, and joined Scunthorpe's Primitive Methodist Church. The wedding caused quite a stir in the local press, and was even filmed by the local cinema. A large crowd, mainly of women, gathered, packing out the 800-seat church and spilling out onto the street. "There was some disorder", one paper reported, "but the minister in charge speedily got the assembly in better terms, so there was no outburst of that ill-feeling which was expected by some." One of Salim's fellow missioners from Yorkshire addressed the congregation, the paper continued, and "in a few earnest words spoke of the high character and integrity of the bridegroom. He was a real man in every sense, and he had known him for 20 years. To those who had been attracted there by the unusual nature of the proceedings, he would remind them of the fact that Moses married an Ethiopian, as recorded in Numbers xii, and that God punished his sister Miriam for her opposition to Moses' choice."

Salim lived the rest of his life in Scunthorpe where he became well known and well liked. He built two houses, one of which he named "Gordon Villa", after the general, and the other "Kathish Villa", after his father, Kathiech. When he died in 1946 he had no living relatives in England, so his lawyers contacted the Sudan government to find out whether any of his father's children or their descendants were still alive. The late Gordon Muortat, then a police sergeant-major in Rumbek, was given the task: some children of his sisters were found, and the money of his estate distributed. Descendants of his sisters are still alive and living in Sudan today.

Salim Charles Wilson, or Machar Kathiech, is remembered both in the land where he died and is buried and in the land of his birth. In Scunthorpe stories about Salim Wilson still appear in the local papers. In Warrap he is still known as Machar, the man who went to England and got education.

Further reading:
Douglas H. Johnson, "Salim Wilson: the black evangelist of the north", *Journal of Religion in Africa*
Douglas H. Johnson, "Salim Charles Wilson", *Dictionary of National Biography*
Salim Charles Wilson, *I Was a Slave*

20
SOUTH SUDANESE SOLDIERS:
'ALI JAIFUN, A SHILLUK SOLDIER

South Sudanese have been scattered all over the globe by the recent civil war, but this is not a new phenomenon. In the nineteenth century many South Sudanese were dispersed from their homelands to far away places by war and slavery, and none were scattered more widely than the soldiers conscripted into the Egyptian army.

When Muhammad 'Ali invaded Sudan in 1820 the Pasha hoped to raise an army of slave soldiers with which to conquer an empire of his own. Slaves came from many sources: from government raids into the Ethiopian foothills, the Nuba Mountains and the White Nile valley, but they were also paid as annual tribute by Egypt's northern Sudanese subjects, many of whom – such as the Sha'qiya, Rufa'a and Baggara – accompanied the army on these raids in order to obtain slaves with which to pay their tribute. Egypt's Sudanese battalions were sent far and wide: to present day Ethiopia, Eritrea and Somalia, but also to Crete, Greece and Mexico.

The career of one such soldier, a Shilluk named 'Ali Jaifun (sometimes written Gifoon), was nothing short of extraordinary. Captured as a slave and then conscripted into the Egyptian army in the mid-nineteenth century, his service took him not only to Egypt and Ethiopia, but as far away as Mexico. He was present in all of the major engagements of the Anglo-Egyptian Reconquest of Sudan from 1888 to 1898. As an Adjutant-Major (Sagh kol Aghasi) he was the highest ranking Sudanese soldier in the Egyptian army at the Battle of Omdurman, and he played an important, if over-looked role, in the Fashoda Incident where Britain and France confronted each other over the Nile. We are fortunate that he dictated his memoirs to his commanding officer, who published them in a British magazine in 1896.

'Ali Jaifun was born Lual Maiker in Fashoda, shortly before or at the beginning of the reign of *reth* Nyidhok Nyakwac (c.1838-1859). When he was a young man, already with a wife and child, the Dongolawi freebooter, Muhammad al-Khair, entered Shilluk country at Kaka and began trading in gum and ivory. He hired Shilluk warriors to help him hunt elephants, and for a year Lual was one of these, learning how to ride a horse and possibly even how to shoot a musket. But Muhammad al-Khair tried to seize the northern half of the Shilluk kingdom, urging some of his Shilluk allies to rise up in revolt against *reth* Nyidhok, who was eventually assassinated. During the civil unrest that followed Nyidhok's death the Shilluk themselves undertook a number of raids. Lual was on one of these raids against Baggara in the Nuba Mountains when his force captured a large herd of Baggara cattle but were surprised by a counter attack in which Lual was captured. He was eventually taken to El Obeid where the Baggara paid him to the Egyptian government as part of their annual tribute. It was there that Lual Maiker became 'Ali Jaifun.

Placed in the second battalion of the Fifth Infantry Regiment 'Ali later recalled, "I found Sudanese of every kind among my comrades, but no Shilluk." His unit was sent on punitive expeditions against Taqali and Fungur in the Nuba Mountains, as well as Massawa in present-day Eritrea. Ali was then rotated to Egypt where he spent three years in and around Alexandria serving in cavalry and artillery units. After returning to the infantry 'Ali's battalion was ordered one day in January 1863 to board a ship. "Soldiers ordered on service do not generally trouble their minds much about who their enemy is to be or why there is to be war", 'Ali later recalled, "and we were no exception to the general rule." The ship was French, and the battalion was bound for Mexico, on loan to the French Emperor Napoleon III in his attempt to carve out a new central American empire.

Landing in the Mexican port of Vera Cruz the battalion was reorganized, rearmed and rekitted along French lines. They had to learn French drill under the instruction of a colonel of an Algerian Zouave regiment, "which was a matter of some difficulty", 'Ali remembered, "for our instructors spoke nothing but French, of which we did not understand a word. After a few days, however, a sergeant and a corporal of Algerian sharpshooters were attached to each company, and their Arabic, though different from our own, soon made matters easy."

The battalion stayed in Mexico for four years, earning high praise from the French, despite the ultimate failure of this imperial venture. The battalion then returned to Egypt via France, where 'Ali was promoted bash shawish (company sergeant-major) and the battalion were paraded in Paris in front of Napoleon III. Each soldier received a Mexican campaign medal, but 'Ali was also awarded the *Médaille Militaire* (Military Medal), a decoration created by the emperor and awarded to non-commissioned officers and enlisted men who distinguished themselves by acts of bravery in action against an enemy force. Napoleon III pinned this medal on 'Ali's tunic himself, and "whenever I was wearing this decoration in the streets of Paris, guards and sentries presented arms as I passed." Quite a change in fortunes for a slave paid in tax.

The men of the battalion were distributed throughout the army on their return to Egypt in order to spread their experience of serving in a modern European army to other units. From the mid-1860s to the early 1880s 'Ali served in garrisons in what is now Eritrea and the Eastern Sudan. He was on the Ethiopian frontier when the Mahdiya broke out, and he was part of the besieged garrison of Kassala that held out until after the fall of Khartoum and the death of the Mahdi in 1885. The garrison commander then decided to surrender, but Ali was among a band of soldiers who escaped to Massawa and made his way to back to Egypt.

Egypt was now under British occupation and control, and the Egyptian army was being reformed under British officers. They very quickly raised a number of Sudanese battalions for permanent duty on Egypt's frontiers with the Mahdist state. 'Ali was first recruited into the 10th Sudanese battalion but in 1888 was promoted yuzbashi (captain) and put in charge of number two company of the 12th Sudanese, in which unit he served with distinction until his death. Just before the re-conquest of Sudan began in 1896 he told his commanding officer, "such as I am, I shall serve the Government as long as my horse will carry me, and if I live to see No. 2 Company of the 12th Sudanese behave as I hope and know they will when the great day comes at Omdurman, then I shall be ready to go, and Ali Gifoon will not perhaps have lived for nothing."

Figure 4: Officers of the 12th Sudanese Battalion in 1888
'Ali Jaifun is sitting second from the left in the second row
(Source: SAD.A89/44, G.G. Hunter collection, Durham University Library)

'Ali certainly did live to see the 12th perform at Omdurman, but he had a further contribution to make after the battle. A French force under Captain Marchand had travelled overland from Senegal and occupied the old Egyptian post of Fashoda (now Kodok) on the White Nile. Kitchener, the British commander-in-chief of the Egyptian Army, sailed up river in a flotilla with two battalions of Sudanese infantry, many of whom were Shilluk. Detached from the 12th for special duty in this expedition was Adjutant-Major 'Ali Jaifun, who became one of the main intermediaries between the Egyptian force and the Shilluk of Fashoda, persuading the *reth* (king), who had signed a treaty with Marchand, that the Egyptians were the superior force. Did he wear his French Mexican and Military Medals, along with his other campaign medals? And if he did, what must have Marchand's thoughts been when confronted with this Sudanese soldier who had once been decorated by the French emperor himself?

'Ali was promoted to the rank of Bimbashi (Major) – a rank previously reserved for British and Egyptian officers – at the end of 1898. He died in Berber in 1899 and was buried with full military honours. But what of his descendants? He had a child whom he left behind in Shilluk country when he was captured as a slave. Are there any descendants of Lual Maiker still alive? And what of any family he might have had while serving as a soldier elsewhere in Sudan and Egypt? Are the descendants of 'Ali Jaifun still living in Berber, or even Morada in Omdurman? The story of 'Ali Jaifun is not yet complete.

Further reading:
    Richard Hill and Peter Hogg, *A Black Corps d'Élite: an Egyptian Sudanese conscript battalion with the French army in Mexico, 1863-1867, and its survivors in subsequent African history*
    Ronald L. Lamothe, *Slaves of Fortune: Sudanese soldiers and the River War, 1896-98*
    Machell, P., "Memoirs of a Sudanese soldier (Ali Effendi Gifoon)", *Cornhill Magazine*

21
SOUTH SUDANESE SOLDIERS: WHO WON THE BATTLE OF OMDURMAN?

In October 1952 the newly established Egyptian Free Officers' government came to an understanding with representatives of the northern Sudanese parties on the terms of Sudan's future self-government and self-determination (chapter 3). South Sudanese parliamentarians had been excluded from this meeting and protested against the amended terms of the self-government statute submitted by Egypt in November, which removed certain safeguards for the South previously agreed by northern and southern members of the Legislative Assembly. Paulo Logali, soon to be a co-founder of the all-Southern Liberal Party (and father of late Hilary Paul Logali), addressed an urgent telegram to Prime Minister Winston Churchill. "Southern Sudan flatly reject Sudan Constitution as amended Cairo", he asserted. "As human beings Southern peoples determined decide their future …you fought Battle of Omdurman to save Sudan and earnestly hope you not help sell us."

Implicit in this reference to the founding event of the Condominium, and Churchill's role in it, is the liberation of the Sudan from tyranny and slavery which was used to justify the re-conquest of the whole of the former Egyptian Sudan, and the imminent betrayal of those on whose behalf the battle was allegedly fought as the Condominium on which it was built now came to an end. The victors of Omdurman were, in Churchill's own words, about to "scuttle".

But who won the Battle of Omdurman? Popular writing and films seem clear on this question. Alexander Korda's 1939 "The Four Feathers", filmed on the battlefield of Karrari plains with the British garrison and Sudan Defence Force as extras, show the battle as won solely by a thin khaki line of British infantry. In the 1972 film "Young Winston", based in part on Churchill's *The River War*, the battle was won by the British artillery and Churchill's 21st Lancers. *Wikipedia* lists the combatants as "Great Britain" and "Sudan", and declares it "a decisive British victory".

A decisive victory it surely was, but the Battle of Omdurman was nowhere so simple as it is often portrayed. Not only was the British contingent a minority of the Anglo-Egyptian force, the most decisive actions of the battle were won by Egyptian and Sudanese soldiers. Yet that significant contribution has been nearly written out of history. In the two most critical episodes of the battle it was Sudanese soldiers who helped to secure the Anglo-Egyptian victory.

The Egyptian Army in those days included several battalions of Sudanese infantry, recruited "for life" from the slave riflemen who had formed the backbone of the old Egyptian garrison in Sudan before the Mahdiya. They included men like 'Ali Jaifun and 'Abd al-Latif Ahmed (the father of 'Ali 'Abd al-Latif) and came from southern Sudan, the Nuba Mountains, Dar Funj and Darfur – those same regions from which the SPLA later gathered its recruits. The Sudanese infantry battalions were frontline troops, garrisoned on Egypt's frontier with the Mahdist state. They even formed the front rank of the Egyptian Camel Corps.

The Reconquest of Sudan began in 1896, and during the next two years the battles were fought almost entirely by Egyptian and Sudanese soldiers with only nominal participation by British units garrisoned in Egypt. When the final push on Omdurman began in 1898 the invasion was reinforced by more British units – two brigades of infantry, some artillery and one cavalry regiment. Despite these reinforcements the British contingent constituted only about a third of the total force. The correspondents writing for the British papers accompanied the British units, and since many were serving officers in the army (Lieutenant Churchill wrote for *The Morning Post*) it is not surprising that the action of British soldiers were recorded in the popular press far more extensively than the Egyptians.

The battle of Omdurman was fought on the Karrari plains north of the Mahdist capital. The Anglo-Egyptian force established their base with the Nile to their backs, in between the Karrari hills to the north and Jebel Surkab to the south. The battle began early on the morning of 2 September 1898 when two divisions of the Mahdist army tried to flank the Anglo-Egyptian force by seizing the Karrari hills, only to find them defended by the entire Egyptian Mounted Brigade consisting of cavalry, camel corps, and horse artillery. While another division tried to assault the Anglo-Egyptian line, the mounted brigade drew their attackers away from the field in a fighting retreat. The Sudanese troopers of the Camel Corps provided the first firing line as their Egyptian comrades withdrew, then fell back under their covering fire. The whole force repeated the process, withdrawing further north along the river until the gunboats of the Egyptian flotilla came to their aid and blasted the two Mahdist divisions to a halt, allowing the mounted troops to return to the main force.

Figure 5: Sudanese soldiers of Macdonald's Brigade await the Ansar attack
(Source: Renée Bull, *Black and White War Albums: Omdurman*)

By this time the first Mahdist assault had disintegrated under the combined fire of Egyptian, Sudanese and British rifle, machine-gun and artillery fire. General Kitchener, the commander of the Anglo-Egyptian force, then ordered an advance on Omdurman, with the two British brigades and the Second and Third Egyptian brigades following the Nile and swinging round the eastern spur of Jebel Surkab. The First Egyptian Brigade under general Macdonald (a Scottish soldier who had risen in the ranks from private to major general), composed of the 2nd Egyptian battalion and 9th, 10th, and 11th Sudanese battalions – the oldest Sudanese units in the Egyptian army – followed behind, exposed on the Karrari plain. What Kitchener did not realize, because the British cavalry regiment, the 21st Lancers, had failed to scout the area, was that the main Mahdist force, the Khalifa Abdallahi's own Black Flag division, was deployed behind Jebel Surkab, poised to attack.

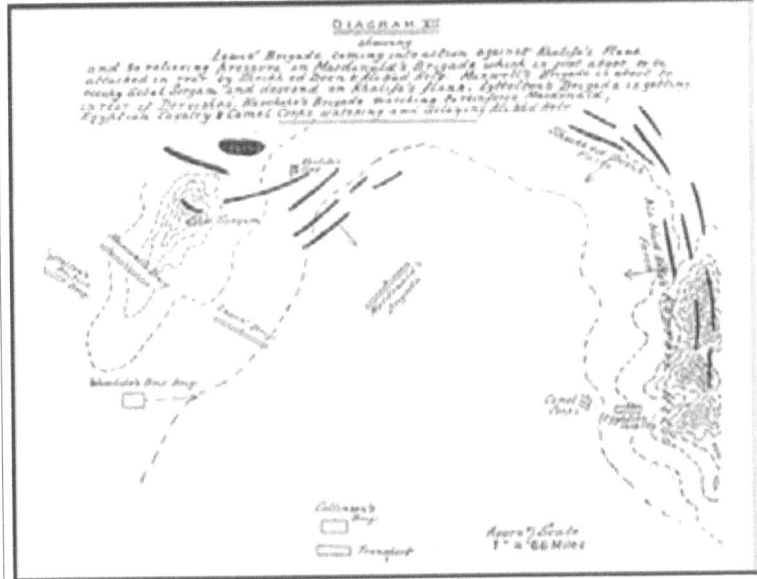

Figure 6: Macdonald's Brigade exposed to attacks on two fronts
(Source: "An Officer", *Sudan Campaigns, 1896-1899*)

When the Black Flag division rushed round the western spur of Jebel Surkab and onto the Karrari plains the First Brigade, considerably outnumbered, advanced in line while under fire to repel the attackers. Initially they were unsupported by any other unit and faced overwhelming odds on their own. Soon the Second Egyptian Brigade – which included three more Sudanese battalions – secured Jebel Surkab and fired down on the Black Flags's flank, with the Third Brigade eventually also lending their support. Thus the attack by the main force of the Khalifa's army was met in the field entirely by Sudanese and Egyptian soldiery.

As the attack began to falter, but before it was completely broken, the two Mahdist divisions that had been drawn off the field by the Mounted Brigade returned to the Karrari hills and threatened the First Brigade's flank. When they began their charge the battalions changed position: the 2nd Egyptians were left to finish off the Black Flag while the three Sudanese battalions, now joined by the Camel Corps, re-deployed to meet the new threat. The English Lincolnshire regiment had been sent to the First Brigade's aid, but by the time they arrived, as the official battle report later recorded, the Sudanese and Egyptians had broken this second attack. The Egyptian Cavalry, who had been hovering on the Mahdist flank, then charged to complete the route.

So what were Lieutenant Winston Churchill and the 21^{St} Lancers doing all this time? They had been sent ahead of the main force to cut off the Khalifa Abdullahi's retreat and attempt his capture, but they were decoyed into an ambush, charging a thin line of riflemen only to discover a larger unit hidden behind them in a khor. Charging through this mass of spear and swordsmen the Lancers reached the opposite bank of the khor, dismounted and fired their carbines, dispersing their enemies.

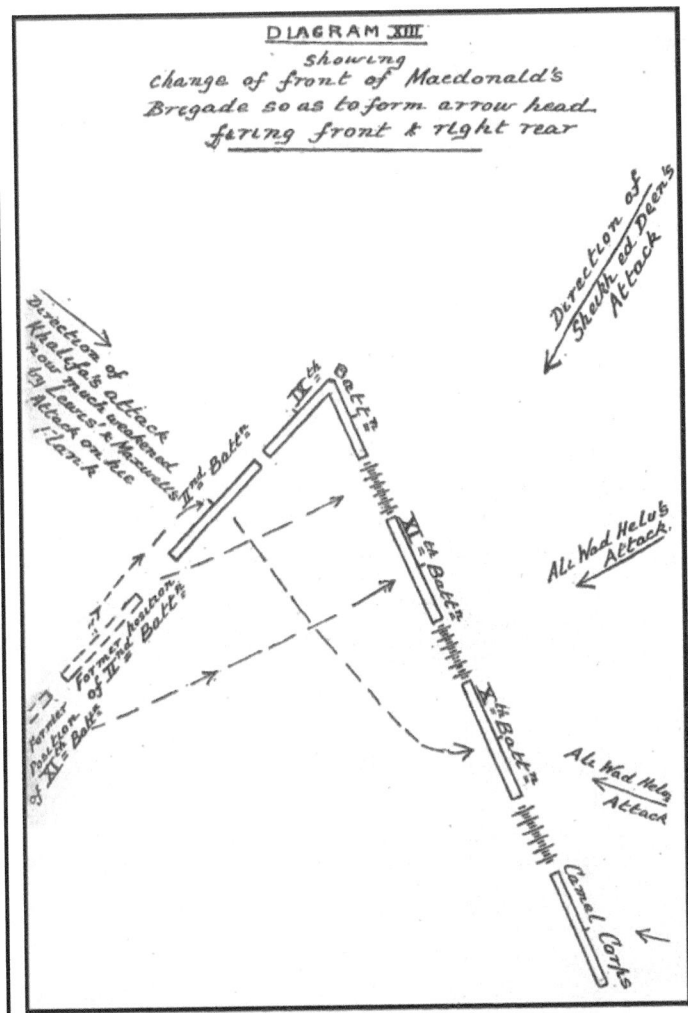

Figure 7: Macdonald's Brigade repels attacks on two fronts
(Source: "An Officer", *Sudan Campaigns, 1896-1899*)

But this local victory was achieved at a high cost in soldiers and horses killed and wounded. The 21st Lancers were too battered to take any further significant part in the battle. It was said after the battle that the Egyptian cavalry was far too experienced to have fallen for this trick that deceived the English cavalry. And it was left to the Egyptian cavalry to attempt to complete the

English cavalry's orders to prevent the Khalifa's escape. They nearly succeeded, entering Omdurman at one side just as the Khalifa escaped out the opposite side.

So the answer to the question, "who won the battle of Omdurman" is more complicated than might be expected. Yes, the British commanders – Kitchener, Macdonald, and the others – won the battle through their leadership, but the soldiers who bore the brunt of the fighting, who were responsible for winning the most important episodes in the battle, were the Sudanese and Egyptians.

You wouldn't know that from the way the battle has been written about for more than a century. Churchill naturally wrote up the events to which he was an eyewitness, but at the same time he denigrated the contribution of the soldiers of the Egyptian army. Later writers have quoted extensively or paraphrased his vivid description and often followed his lead in exaggerating the importance of the 21st Lancers and the Lincolnshire regiment, while ignoring the 9th, 10th and 11th Sudanese battalions. So if the Khalifa's rule was a tyranny from which the Sudan was saved, Paulo Logali was being excessively generous in crediting Churchill with that salvation. It would have been only fair had Churchill returned the compliment by acknowledging the role of South Sudanese, Nuba, Fur and Funj in that same salvation.

Further reading:
    Ronald L. Lamothe, *Slaves of Fortune: Sudanese soldiers and the River War, 1896-98*

22
SOUTH SUDANESE SOLDIERS: 'ALI 'ABD AL-LATIF AND THE WHITE FLAG LEAGUE

After the Addis Ababa Agreement was signed in the 1970s, 'Ali 'Abd al-Latif, a former Sudanese army officer, was a celebrated symbol of Sudanese unity as a "Southerner" and a Muslim who had championed Sudanese nationalism. This is still how he is remembered by many Sudanese. But both 'Ali 'Abd al-Latif's background and his life were more complicated than that. While after his death he was hailed as the symbol of Sudanese nationalism, during his life he was repudiated by Sudanese nationalists.

'Ali's parents were slaves in the town of al-Khandaq, south of Dongola. His father, 'Abd al-Latif Ahmad, was a Nuba, and his mother, al-Sabr Zayn, was a Dinka Rek. The two were caught up in 'Abd al-Rahman al-Nujumi's fatal invasion of Egypt in 1888 when 'Abd al-Latif was impressed into the *jihadiyya*, the riflemen of the Mahdist army and, after al-Nujumi's defeat at Tushki, joined a Sudanese battalion in the Egyptian army composed of ex-slaves from the Nuba Mountains, the southern Sudan, Darfur and Dar Funj. 'Ali 'Abd al-Latif was born some time in the early 1890s while his father was garrisoned in Wadi Halfa, then part of Egypt, serving first with the 13th and then with the 15th Sudanese Battalion. So, strictly speaking, 'Ali 'Abd al-Latif was not a "Southerner", having been born in an Egyptian military garrison and tracing patrilineal descent to the Nuba Mountains and matrilineal descent to the South.

'Abd al-Latif participated in the re-conquest of Sudan in 1896-99, rising to the rank of corporal, eventually retiring to an ex-soldier colony near Dueim. His son 'Ali decided that Dueim offered few opportunities for education so he sought out one of his maternal uncles in Khartoum, Rihan 'Abdallah, a retired Dinka army officer from 'Abd al-Latif's 15th battalion then living in Burri. With Rihan's patronage 'Ali was educated first at a local Koranic school, then at Gordon Memorial College, and finally entered the Military School, where he graduated in 1913, being awarded the Sirdar's Medal as the best cadet in his year.

On graduation 'Ali was commissioned a Second Lieutenant in the 11th Battalion and was stationed at Talodi in the Nuba Mountains. After the conquest of Darfur in 1916 he was transferred to the 9th Battalion and was based in El Fasher. In 1918 he was promoted to the rank of First Lieutenant and subsequently served in Rumbek where he was appointed mamur in Shambe. There he had a sideline in elephant hunting and ivory trading which enabled him to buy two houses in Khartoum. Finally he was transferred to the 14th Battalion in Wad Medani.

'Ali 'Abd al-Latif straddled two very different social strata of Sudanese society. One was the lower class ex-slave community of his parents, the retired soldiers who provided the tailors, carpenters and artisans residing in the malakiyas of Sudan's towns. The other was the rising middle-class of the mainly Northern Sudanese educated "effendiya" who provided the junior officers and bureaucrats employed by the Anglo-Egyptian government. Among the latter 'Ali became known as a rising intellectual. He was a member of the executive committee of the Omdurman Graduates' Club (which later became the nucleus of the politically active Graduates' Congress in the 1930s). He was well read, kept abreast of the Egyptian newspapers, and counted among his friends Muhammad Neguib, an Egyptian officer serving in Sudan who would later be the figurehead of the Free Officers' coup and Egypt's first president.

The British authorities were increasingly suspicious of this "de-tribalized" class of ex-slaves, who did not fit into the tribal structures being reconstructed throughout Sudan, could not be subordinated to the hierarchy of tribal notables then being co-opted into the rural administration of the country, and who had divided loyalties. As a soldier in a Sudanese battalion 'Ali was an officer in the Egyptian Army, holding a commission from the King of Egypt, not the King of Britain. 'Ali's loyalties, therefore, lay with Egypt as well as Sudan. In 1922 he was dismissed from the army and imprisoned for one year for trying to publish a "seditious" document entitled "Claims of the Sudanese Nation". In it he asserted the right of the Sudanese people to choose between Egypt and Britain as guardians until they reached the stage of independence, demanded the expansion of education and the appointment of Sudanese to the administration, and criticised the pro-British religious and tribal notables, such as 'Abd al-Rahman al-Mahdi and 'Ali al-Mirghani, as "representing no one but themselves". 'Ali's trial and imprisonment for a year made him a national figure.

After his release 'Ali became prominent in nationalist circles, but his activities also revealed splits in the nationalist ideology. Within the leadership of League of Sudanese Union some advocated a "union" between Sudanese, while others urged union between Egypt and Sudan. When one of the League's leaders published a book of poetry dedicated to "the Noble Arab People", 'Ali objected, saying instead that the dedication should have been to "the Noble Sudanese People". This revealed a division within the League between traditional and progressive ideas about Sudanese identity.

It was shortly after this that the White Flag League was founded in 1924, supplanting the League of Sudanese Union as the leading nationalist organization. But even its foundation revealed how elusive unity between Sudanese was. Many of the founders of the White Flag League were sons of tribal notables, but they could not agree among themselves who should lead the new party. Finally 'Ali 'Abd al-Latif suggested, "What do you think if I become the president of this society, though I don't claim I am the noblest of you?" acknowledging his slave ancestry. "What do you think if I assume responsibility and become the president of the White Flag League?" 'Ali was acclaimed president unanimously. From that point on he became known as Al-Za'im, "The Leader".

It was due to 'Ali 'Abd al-Latif's leadership that the White Flag League was able to attract many of the urban working class in its demonstrations in the Three Towns in 1924, as well as the cadets in the Military School, representing both the lower and upper ends of Sudanese social strata. But it was not just the British who saw 'Ali as dangerous, imprisoning him shortly after the demonstrations began. The tribal and religious notables working closely with the colonial administration also saw him as a threat. The influential paper *al-Hadarat al-Sudan* complained of the country being humiliated "when the most insignificant, the meanest people who occupy no important position in society dared to demonstrate". Only the leaders of the tribes, it went on to claim, "have the rights to talk about state politics", asking dismissively "to which tribe does this 'Ali 'Abd al-Latif, who has become famous recently, belong?"

'Ali was already serving a three-year prison sentence when Sudanese soldiers in Khartoum mutinied in 1925. The crushing of that mutiny led to the suppression of the White Flag League, and though 'Ali had no direct hand in the mutiny, his sentence was extended and he was sent to prison in Wau. But even when his sentence expired he was kept in prison until 1938, when he was sent to Egypt and detained in a mental hospital. He died there in 1948.

The aims of the White Flag League were ambiguous, advocating at one and the same time the "Unity of the Nile Valley" and "Sudan for the Sudanese". 'Ali was genuinely influenced by and sympathized with the Egyptian nationalists. But given his earlier manifesto declaring Sudan's right to independence it is possible that his advocacy of unity with Egypt was tactical, using an alliance with Egypt to remove the British first, before then achieving independence.

Just as 'Ali was rejected by the country's notables in the 1920s, he was still not embraced by the generation of nationalists who campaigned for independence in the 1940s. In 1946, two years before 'Ali died, and only a few months before arguing strenuously for unity at the Juba Conference, Judge Shingeitti, a former member of the League of Sudanese Union and now an Ummah Party politician, spoke with a British minister. "Shangetti boasted that the Sudanese had come from Arabia," the minister recorded. "He spoke very contemptuously of Abdel Latif (now in an insane asylum). He said his mother was a negress, his father was unknown, and that he, Latif, had at one time collected old tins from barracks." Sudanese nationalism had not lost its racial tinge.

Figure 8: Banner of 'Ali 'Abd al-Latif and John Garang displayed outside the Khartoum Hilton, 2005 (photo: Douglas H. Johnson)

Yet, now 'Ali 'Abd al-Latif continues to inspire people over a century after his birth. For some he is the embodiment of the elusive "New Sudan". After the CPA was signed his portrait was prominently displayed along with John Garang's in the streets of Khartoum.

Further reading:
    Yoshiko Kurita, *'Ali 'Abd al-Latif wa Thawra 1924* [in Arabic: Ali Abd al-Latif and the Revolution of 1924]
    Elena Vezzadini, *Lost Nationalism: Memory, Insurgency, and Revolutionary Departures in Colonial Sudan*

23
SOUTH SUDANESE ABROAD: THE NUBIS

The civil war of 1983-2005 saw the dispersal of South Sudanese around the world. Hundreds of thousands were scattered into internally-displaced centres in Sudan and refugee camps throughout Northeast Africa; many thousands settled further abroad, in Australia, Europe, Canada, the United States and elsewhere; thousands were abducted as slaves to the north. Many thousands still live abroad.

This is not the first time that South Sudan's population has been dispersed by war and slavery. In the nineteenth century many were taken to the north, Egypt and beyond. While slavery took them, not all ended up as slaves in the conventional sense. Many thousands ended up in the Egyptian army – the men as soldiers, the women as their wives (chapters 20 & 21). The garrisons formed large permanent communities of men, women and children – the beginnings of the malakiyas of modern South Sudanese towns. One such network of garrisons in Equatoria managed to survive the wars of the Mahdiya and escape into East Africa. These were the ancestors of today's Nubi communities in Uganda and Kenya.

In the 1880s the governor of the Egyptian province of Equatoria was a German, Eduard Schnitzer, better known by his Turkish name and title, Emin Pasha. The soldiers of his army came from all over South Sudan, but many also came from the Nuba Mountains, Darfur, Dar Funj, and even what are now Ethiopia and the Congo. When the Ansar of the Mahdi advanced south Emin and his garrisons retreated further up the Nile, past Nimule to Dufile and Wadelai in present day Uganda. There in 1888 Emin was reached by an expedition led by the American adventurer, Henry Morton Stanley, who then "rescued" Emin and took him and some of his men to Zanzibar.

Only a few accompanied Emin and Stanley. The majority were left behind in Uganda under the command of a Sudanese officer, Salim Bey Matar, and he established a garrison in northern Uganda. It was there that in 1892 they met Captain (later Lord) Lugard who had come to secure the commercial interests of the Imperial British East African Company (IBEAC). Lugard needed an army with which to establish his control, and Salim Bey had a ready-made army. Lugard persuaded Salim and his soldiers to temporarily serve under with the IBEAC, pending permission from the Khedive of Egypt, whom they still regarded as their sovereign and master. In the meantime Lugard redistributed them around different forts within Uganda and along the road between Uganda and the coast.

By this time Egypt was under the control of Britain and had abandoned Sudan. The Egyptian government did not want the financial liability of retaining these Sudanese soldiers in their service: of paying several years back-salary, or of paying for their repatriation to Egypt, so they gladly granted permission for the IBEAC to take them on as their private army. When Britain formally took over Uganda these soldiers became a new regiment known as the Uganda Rifles, a unit recruited entirely from Sudanese. In the early twentieth century these Sudanese soldiers formed the nucleus of the Ugandan and Kenyan battalions of what became the King's African Rifles.

It is misleading to think of these communities as consisting entirely, or even mostly, of soldiers. Of the 10,000 persons Salim Bey brought over to Lugard only about 800 were soldiers. The rest were their wives and children, the wives and children of deceased soldiers, as well as slaves the soldiers had captured. For the first two decades of the twentieth century the King's African Rifles continued to recruit from these communities, and very large settlements of Sudanese grew up in Bomba in Uganda and Kibera in Kenya.

If these were South Sudanese, how did they get the name "Nubi"? One story that is often told is that when Salim Bey arrived in Kampala the Kabaka of Buganda asked him his tribe, and he replied "Nuba", because he was from the Nuba Mountains. We don't in fact know whether Salim Bey was a Nuba, but the term is much older than that. Nuba was not originally an ethnic label. In the Nile Basin both *bilad an-Nuba* (Nubia) and *bilad as-Sudan* (the Sudan) described areas from which Egypt and other states in the region took slaves. To be a Nuba in relation to either Egypt or the kingdom of Sinnar on the Blue Nile meant essentially the same thing: one was either a slave or provided slaves to the state. "Nubian" slaves in Egypt came from virtually any part of Sudan, even if the Nubian speakers (Danaqla, Ja'liyyin, etc.) merely provided slaves in tribute or trade. The "Nuba" soldiers of Sinnar were slaves captured from the Ethiopian foothills as well as from present day Nuba Mountains. Slave regiments in the Egyptian army, made up increasingly of southern Sudanese, continued to be called "Nubian" regiments into the late nineteenth century. This is the origin of the term "Nubi". In fact the ex-slave soldier communities in East Africa were called both "Nubi" and "Sudanese" interchangeably throughout the first half of the twentieth century.

The Nubi communities of East Africa shared much in common with the malakiyas of South Sudan. Both were composed largely of discharged soldiers and their families. Both professed Islam, and both spoke languages derived from the military Arabic of the Sudanese battalions in the Egyptian army. Ki-Nubi, the language of the East African Nubis, took on many characteristics of the surrounding languages but retained a substantial core of Arabic vocabulary. The Arabic of the Sudanese malakiyas, what is now called "Juba Arabic", was also known as "Nubi Arabic" in the early twentieth century.

Being either Nubi or Sudanese in East Africa in the early-to-mid twentieth century was a flexible identity. While many Nubis trace their descent to one of Salim Bey's soldiers, the Nubi communities absorbed a number of individuals from neighbouring societies. In northern Uganda the expression "becoming Nubi," described a process whereby persons from rural areas settled in the towns, adopted Muslim names and dress, and began speaking Ki-Nubi. The same expression was used in Equatoria during Sudan's first civil war to describe people moving out of the war zones of the rural areas and adopting the protective camouflage of Muslim names and dress in Juba.

Other persons joined the Nubi communities in other ways. One Kenyan woman I worked with in Operation Lifeline Sudan in the 1990s explained to me that her grandfather was a Swahili trader from the coast who came to Juba for several years in the 1920s and married a Bari woman there. When he returned to Kenya he settled his wife and their children in Kibera. "You see", my colleague explained to me, "I'm too dark to be Swahili, so I'm Nubi."

Throughout the colonial period in East Africa the Nubis, or Sudanese as they preferred to call themselves then, asserted a separate identity from their neighbours, and a special relationship to the colonial government based on their history of military service. Their biggest battle was over their right to settle in Kibera. As early as 1904 Sudanese ex-soldiers were settled some distance from Nairobi in an area they named "Kibra" or "Kibera", from the Arabic *ghabra*, meaning forest or bush. By the 1930s, however, Nairobi had expanded out towards Kibera, and the city wanted to move the Sudanese elsewhere. The Sudanese objected on the grounds that the settlement had been granted them in perpetuity by the military authorities in lieu of a pension. Even though this had been the practice throughout the period of colonial conquest and pacification the Kenya Colony government refused to accept this argument.

The dispute went on for years. The Sudanese asserted their loyalty to the "King-Emperor" and claimed they had been brought to East Africa while serving His Majesty's Government. And they asked, "Who brought the Sudanese to Kenya and for what reason? Has their work been good or bad? Where is the compensation for those who lost their lives serving the British Government and where are the widows and orphans?"

It was the Mau Mau Emergency of the 1950s that helped to secure for the Sudanese their tenure in Kibera when the Kenyan government decided that the forced removal of so large a population could not be undertaken for security reasons. Sudanese independence and approaching Kenyan independence forced the Sudanese to rethink their argument that they were a foreign nationality within Kenya, and from the 1950s on the term "Sudanese" was dropped in favour of "Nubi", with Nubi being asserted as a tribal, not national, identity. The final irony is that the Nubis' earlier arguments have at last been accepted by the post-independence Kenyan government, but as a way of disenfranchising them. The Kenya government has concluded that the Nubi claim to a special status based on their origin outside of East Africa proves that they are foreigners and not Kenyan citizens. The Nubis have appealed, giving their old arguments a post-colonial twist. No longer do they claim to have been willingly brought to Kenya while loyally serving His Majesty's Government; instead they now claim to have been "forcibly moved" to Kenya by the British, an experience consistent with a different kind of servitude from the one that brought them to East Africa.

Further readering:
> Douglas H. Johnson, "Tribe or nationality? The Sudanese diaspora and the Kenyan Nubis", *Journal of Eastern African Studies*

24
SOUTH SUDAN'S EARLY LEADERS: STANISLAUS PAYSAMA, SLAVE AND MINISTER

One of South Sudan's earliest political leaders, Stanislaus Abdallahi Paysama – or "Uncle Stans" as he was later known – was not originally from South Sudan. He was from Darfur, and how he came to live and rise to prominence in South Sudan is part of the history that connects those two regions. We know something of his early life from the autobiography, *How a Slave Became A Minister*, which he wrote and dictated before his death in 1987. It was later printed in Khartoum, and all quotations cited below are taken from it.

Stanislaus was born Abdullahi Kujuk Usama Haroun in the south-west Darfur village of Nyerle around 1905, during the reign of sultan Ali Dinar. His father was both a blacksmith and a faki. When Stanislaus was about nine years old his father and two uncles were killed by Arab raiders who attacked the village. Stanislaus was separated from his family and eventually fell in with a group of Beni Halaba, who were themselves fleeing a Fur counter-attack, and who promised to return him to his family. But then he was captured by a slave-dealer who specialized in selling young boys and girls. By a series of lucky chances Stanislaus managed to get to a police post at Kafia Kingi in Bahr al-Ghazal where he was finally freed by an Egyptian mamur (a junior official, assistant to the British Inspector).

At Kafia Kingi Stanislaus was looked after by a Fur woman, also a freed slave, married to a policeman. In all some seventy freed slave boys and girls from Darfur groups such as Borgo, Wadai and Daju were gathered in Kafia Kingi. Some were recruited into the police and army, but Stanislaus was among a group who were sent to Wau for schooling. There he was taught English and Religion by the Catholic fathers, and Arabic and arithmetic by an Egyptian school master with the very Coptic Christian name of Boutrus Ghali. His fellow students and friends were mostly Azande, among who was James Tembura (later a fellow representative from Bahr al-Ghazal to the 1948 Legislative Assembly, and father of Joseph James Tembura, a president of the High Executive Council of the Southern Region). It was there he was received into the Catholic Church and given the name Stanislaus (he later admitted that he did not know where the name Paysama came from). He stayed at the school in Wau from 1914 to 1918, when he was sent to Khartoum to train as a teacher. He returned to Wau and taught school there from 1921 to 1926. After falling out with the missionaries he joined the government service as a clerk, serving in Wau, Raga, Yirol and Rumbek.

In 1943 Stanislaus sat for the Sudan Civil Service examination, the first graduate of a southern school to do so. On passing with high marks he was sent to Khartoum to work in the British civil secretary's office. It was in this capacity that he attended the 1947 Juba Conference, not as a delegate, but as the civil secretary's clerk (chapter 2). His account of the behind-the-scenes negotiations outside of the conference is very different from what has become the semi-official record.

From his work in government service Stanislaus had come to know a number of the participants at the Juba Conference, both southern and northern. When the conference had reached a deadlock the civil secretary, James Robertson, instructed Stanislaus to issue tickets to everyone to return to their homes. Stanislaus then went to see Judge Shingeiti who exclaimed angrily, "Look, ya Stanislaus, your people are so dull, so stupid that they cannot understand how thing are getting on. Why should not the Southerners join the Assembly together with their northern friends? They will sit down there like anybody else, and they will put forward their case. The Northerners should listen to it. We are all Sudanese."

Stanislaus then went to talk to the southern delegates, who held a meeting of their own with about two hundred southern clerks and junior officials. The meeting lasted until two o'clock in the morning. Finally, Chier Rehan, one of the Dinka chiefs at the conference, spoke, saying, "Gentlemen, we now have stayed too long. Why should we be afraid of the Northerners? What I know is that Stanislaus will not betray us and, if anything happens, if the Northerners want to make injustice to us, well, we have young children, young men: they will take up the response and fight them; they are men like ourselves." Another Dinka chief, Deng Tong, seconded that sentiment, proclaiming, "Let us go to Khartoum and, if necessary, we shall organize the fight to defend ourselves."

Many years later, when Stanislaus read Sir James Robertson's memoir, crediting Shingeiti with persuading the southern delegates to join the Legislative Assembly with a promise of higher wages, he commented, "No...Shingeiti did not say, nor did we say anything about better salaries; we spoke about better living and about our going to the Legislative Assembly."

Stanislaus was one of thirteen Southerners appointed to the Legislative Assembly in 1948, having been selected by the Province Council in Wau. When the Ummah Party brought forward a self-government motion in 1950 Stanislaus led the opposition to it, because he felt not enough had been done to enable the South to participate in self-government on an equal basis. When the first self-government elections were held in 1953 Stanislaus was elected to the Senate, where he became the Leader of the Opposition. He was a co-founder along with Benjamin Lwoki and Buth Diu of the South's first party, the Liberal Party, and was an advocate of federalism. He was appointed Minister of Mechanical Transport in the first independence government in 1956, and he was president of the Liberal Party during the 1957 elections when it and the federalist bloc won all of the South's seats, becoming the third largest group in the new parliament, after the National Union Party and the Ummah Party, neither of whom had a majority.

Had they remained united, the Southerners could have held the balance of power in that parliament.

There was a move in parliament, supported by many northern parliamentarians, to elect Stanislaus prime minister. But divisions among the Southerners prevented that from happening. Because Stanislaus was originally from Darfur many Southerners accused him of being more of a Northerner than a Southerner. They also had disagreements over what type of federation they wanted – Stanislaus advocated something more along the lines of the regional autonomy the South was later given by the Addis Ababa Agreement than full federalism. Fr. Saturnino, Buth Diu and Joseph Oduho all voted against Stanislaus, and the South lost the first chance it had to have one of its own lead the national government.

Disillusioned by southern dis-unity, Stanislaus left politics after the Abboud coup in 1958. When Abboud fell in 1964 he tried to persuade other Southern leaders to form a single party, but the differences between them were too strong, and unity eluded them yet again. After living awhile in Khartoum he retired to Wau, where he died on 28 December 1987, and where he is buried.

In Stanislaus Abdallahi Paysama's life are reflected many of the major events in Sudan's modern history. Divisions in Darfur, which have been repeated on a grander scale today. The persistence of slavery, so that even though he was born a Muslim he was enslaved. The attempt to forge a united nation out of unequal parts, the internal rivalries and divisions that prevented the South as a region from taking a leading role in the nation's development. Belonging to no tribe, he decried tribalism, remarking "I don't know how I could have rendered my services to a particular family, clan or tribe." A devout Catholic, he did not hate Muslims or Northerners, yet he saw the conflict between North and South as fundamentally religious, noting that "the jallabas in the market and the officials in their offices had become religious propagandists. This angered the people. It is stupid of them; they only concentrated on religious matters and neglected the wishes of the people; they did not respect the tribal habits and customs and they did not even respect Christianity." About the future he predicted, "this trouble should continue for generations, if the Northerners think only about religion and nothing about any other thing."

Stanislaus Paysama saw the end of the first civil war, the formation and collapse of the Southern Region, and the beginning of the second civil war. Before he died he recorded his reflections. "Now can the South be united again?" he asked. "I don't see how", was his first pessimistic answer to his own question. But then he went on to say, "This should be easy to do if the regional government is returned back to Juba. It could be very difficult, but if the Southerners realize their mistake, they study it carefully and try to resist corruption and tribalism, I think there will be progress. But this will take time." If Southerners do study their past carefully, perhaps it won't take as long as Stanislaus predicted.

Further reading:
    Fr. Dellagiacoma (ed.), *How a Slave became a Minister: autobiography of sayyed Stanislaus Abdallahi Paysama*

25
SOUTH SUDAN'S EARLY LEADERS: LOGALIS

One of the surprises of returning to Juba after so many years was to find a first class hotel and restaurant named after someone I knew – Logali's. There is a picture in the reception of Hilary Paul (whom I knew), and his father, Paulo Logali (about whom I had read), but little to explain to the guests what these men did and why we should remember them. Both contributed to the development of the South Sudanese political movement, and each, in his own way, tried to avoid the ethnic divisions of South Sudanese politics.

Logali was not their real name. Logali, or Logale, was a missionary corruption of the Kuku name 'Doggale, meaning "the Giver of Milk". Paulo Logali Wani, who came from a village near Rejaf, was one of the first Bari boys to attend the Church Missionary Society Nugent School in Juba. Paulo was the youngest of three brothers. The eldest, Mori Wani, remained in the village and followed his ancestral religion. The second, Pitia, was converted to Islam by Muslim Baganda missionaries in Mongalla (then the province capital) and took the name Omar Rajab Osman. In the matter of religion the sons of Wani were representative of the choices offered southern Sudanese: to remain with the ancestors or convert to the new religions of Christianity or Islam.

Paulo Logali was one of the first cadre of trained teachers among the Bari and was posted to Kajo-Kaji. He later became a book-keeper in the government in Juba. He kept his ties with the Bari parish as a church councillor and then as its first indigenous Diocesan treasurer. His wife, Maria Meja Swaka, was also a Christian, and her elder brother, Jebedayo (Zebedee) Jada Swaka was ordained as an Anglican priest and became the Reverend Canon Jebedayo Jada Swaka.

When Hilary was born in his mother's village of Nyaing – just north of today's Juba airport – he was given five Bari names – Nyigilo Yugusuk Sule Kulang Kwajok – but was then nicknamed Lokuku ("of Kukuland"), a reminder of his parents' land of origin. In addition to these names his Christian parents had him baptised as Hilary, leading him to comment some years later in his unpublished memoir, "I therefore had no choice but to be born an Anglican."

Paulo Logali's political activism began in the late 1940s, after the 1947 Juba Conference. There were no South Sudanese political parties or organizations at that time, and Paulo was one of a number of educated junior civil servants who formed the Southern Intelligentsia Association in Juba. Stanislaus Paysama was its first chairman, but when he was transferred to Wau Paulo Logali became the chair. It was as chair of the association that Paulo sent his famous telegram to Winston Churchill protesting the 1952 All-Parties Agreement with Egypt.

Following 1952 the Liberal Party was formed out of the old Southern Intelligentsia Association with Stanislaus Paysama as president, Benjamin Lwoki as vice president, Buth Diu as secretary general and Paulo Logali as treasurer.

Paulo was elected a Senator to the first Sudanese parliament where the Liberal Party was the largest block of southern representatives and often acted in alliance with the Ummah opposition. The Ummah Party nominated Paulo Logali for the Governor-General's Council against the pro-Egyptian NUP Siricio Iro Wani, who won. Later, when Stanislaus Paysama lost his cabinet seat the Liberal Party first nominated Paulo Logali to replace him, but had to withdraw the nomination when members from Bahr el-Ghazal claimed that the position should belong to one of them because Paysama was from Bahr el-Ghazal. Similar objections were raised by Upper Nile members when a cabinet place became vacant after independence.

The Liberal Party came to an end with the Abboud coup of 1958 and Paulo Logali returned to Juba. Though he had been admired by many northern parliamentarians with whom he worked, including the later prime minister Muhammad Ahmad Mahjub, none of these former colleagues sent condolences when Paulo suddenly died in Juba in December 1965, at the age of fifty-six. In many ways he had become a forgotten man.

Hilary Paul's introduction to politics overlapped with his father's political career. Hilary was educated throughout the South, attending school at Loka, Atar and Rumbek, finally being one of the first South Sudanese to enter Khartoum University in 1952. His pan-southern education gave him an early sense of South Sudan as a region. This was one reason why his own politics were never tribal and he cooperated with leaders from across the South. He was in Khartoum at the same time his father was in parliament, and Hilary and other southern students used to meet with the Southern parliamentarians in his father's house to discuss politics and policy.

Hilary was no stranger to political agitation. At university he was introduced to Marxist literature and became friends with many Communist students, such as Joseph Ukel Garang, and organized a demonstration of Northern and Southern students against army's activities in the South in 1956. He was to put this experience to good use after the Abboud coup in 1958. By that time Hilary, who had graduated with a University of London BA, was working in the Ministry of Finance in Khartoum. He very soon began organizing an underground movement of younger, educated South Sudanese civil servants, adapting the cell system he had learned from the Communists. Throughout 1958-64 he worked with other leaders such as Darius Bashir, Abel Alier, Isaiah Majok, Gordon Muortat and Dr. Richard Hassan Kalam Sakit, and kept in contact with the exile leaders Aggrey Jaden, Joseph Oduho and William Deng. When Darius Bashir was transferred to Nyala in 1964 Hilary became chairman of the Khartoum cell.

Hilary was in America on a scholarship to Yale University when the Abboud government fell in 1964, and he was called back to Sudan. In Khartoum the underground organization came out in the open as the Southern Front, with Hilary as secretary general and Minister of Works and National Resources in the transitional government. Hilary then led the delegation to Uganda to persuade the Jaden wing of SANU to participate in the Round Table Conference. But the Southern Front refused to take part in the elections of 1965, claiming that it would be impossible to hold free and fair elections in the South at that time, and for the next few years Hilary was out of government and the Southern Front suffered as its members in the South were targeted by the army.

A new coalition government in 1967 brought the Southern Front back into government, with Hilary once again becoming a minister. In the 1968 elections he was elected to parliament to represent the Juba West constituency. As a cabinet minister in 1969 he was imprisoned for a year after Nimeiri's takeover but was brought back into government after the failed Communist coup in Khartoum when Nimeiri needed Southern support. Hilary became Commissioner for Equatoria Province, a position he held at the time of the 1972 Addis Ababa Agreement.

In the early years of the Southern Region Hilary served as Minister of Finance, Economic Planning, Industry and Mining, was assistant secretary general of the Sudan Socialist Union for the Southern Region, was elected to the Regional Assembly and served as Leader of the House and later as Speaker. He was also Chair of the University Council.

Hilary tried to stand outside the parochial politics that eventually engulfed the Southern Region, but it was impossible not to be affected by them. He lost his Juba constituency in 1978 because he was accused of being too close to Abel Alier and the Dinka, but afterwards was then marginalized by the Alier group. Despite this he opposed the Equatorian plan to divide the South. He continued to chair the Juba University Council after Nimeiri abolished the Southern Region and was brought back as Minister of Finance in the Transitional High Executive Council after Nimeiri was overthrown in 1985. But he was disappointed by the lack of unity in the southern Sudanese political associations during the brief parliamentary period and for all intents and purposes his political career was at an end.

Reflecting on the failure of the Southern Region he concluded that one reason the Addis Ababa peace had failed was because South Sudanese lacked the skills and experience to manage such a complex administration effectively. In 1994 he approached some British people who had been involved in the Southern Africa Advanced Education Project that had worked with the African National Council to provide training for South Africans before the end of apartheid and asked if they could set up a similar programme to support a future peace in South Sudan. Working with Lawrence Modi Tombe and the South Sudanese diaspora in the UK "Skills for Southern Sudan" was begun and now, as Skills for South Sudan, is an independent NGO providing training for South Sudanese in various fields and at various levels. Hilary maintained a very active interest in the project up until his death in London in 1998, and the programme stands as a monument to his far-sightedness and his dedication to the future development of South Sudan.

Hilary was buried in Khartoum in 1998. Early in 2011, the year of South Sudan's independence, his remains were flown to Juba for reburial.

Further reading:
    A copy of Hilary Paul Logali's unfinished and unpublished autobiography, on which much of this is based, is kept in the Sudan Archive, University of Durham, United Kingdom.

PLACES

26
WHOSE NAMES ARE ON SOUTH SUDAN'S MAP?

Before the referendum the National Bureau of Statistics began preparing to re-map South Sudan. This was long overdue since the Sudan Survey 1:250,000 maps have not had their topographical information updated since the 1930s, and more recent maps produced by the University of Berne lack "ground truthing" for the identification of local names and sites. In fact the names used on Sudanese maps are hopelessly confused. The reason is simple: Sudan's place names come from a variety of languages: indigenous (living, dead, or forgotten), Arabic, and even English, yet they have been written down using different phonetic systems of English and Arabic, none of which adequately represented vernacular pronunciations of indigenous names.

The Sudan Survey Department was established by the military cartographers of the Egyptian army, and the British officers who began mapping Sudan at the turn of the century used a simplified system for transcribing Egyptian colloquial Arabic into English script. There are significant differences in pronunciation between Egyptian and Sudanese Arabic, one of the most common is the pronunciation of the Arabic consonants "jim" and "qaf". In Egypt "jim" is pronounced as a hard "g", while "qaf" is pronounced much like the English "q". But in Sudanese Arabic "jim" is pronounced as a soft "j" while "qaf" is pronounced as a hard "g". By the 1920s most British officials serving in Sudan in either a military or civil capacity had learned Sudanese colloquial Arabic and were transcribing place names according to the phonetic values they were then hearing. This is why there is no consistency in the writing of some names on the Sudan Survey maps. "G" is written to signify both "qaf" and "jim": Qoz was written Goz, Jamaiza was written Gemmeiza, Mujlad became Muglad, and Jambiel became Gumbiel. Some names appear in alternate spellings on the same map: Khor Ajaj is written both Ajaj and Agag on the Berne Map of Abyei. The writing of the consonant "k" only added to the confusion: thus Wun Rok sometimes appears as Wun Rog.

Things become even more confused when looking at the place names of South Sudan. The first interpreters British officials used were the South Sudanese soldiers serving in the Egyptian army, so some surveys apply Egyptian colloquial transcriptions to vernacular names, and others apply Sudanese colloquial conventions. In many Nilotic languages "p" and "f" are interchangeable, so some maps will have Pul Turuk, Paddoi, or Duk Padiat, while others will have Ful Turuk, Faddoi, and Duk Fadiat. British officials also habitually wrote the Nilotic "c", which is pronounced "ch", as "sh"; thus Machar and Mashar will appear in different places on the same map, and Cith will appear as Shit rather than Chit.

Imposing a combination of English and Arabic phonetic transcriptions on Nilotic names produced some puzzling results. The Shilluk royal capital of Pacodo became Fashoda; thus losing its meaning of "The Place (or village) of the Hornless Cow". Pangak, "The Place of the Pied Crow (gak)", became Fanjak, which is meaningless in either Dinka or Nuer. Some changes were even more bizarre. The village of the powerful northern Bahr el-Ghazal Dinka chief, Awutiak, was transformed into "Chak Chak". Even though a system of orthography for South Sudanese vernacular languages was devised and adopted for educational purposes in the 1920s, this was never applied to Sudanese cartography, and these inconsistencies and peculiarities continue to appear on many modern maps.

Another layer of confusion has been applied on post-independence maps when all place names were written first in Arabic, and then transcribed using a Modern Literary Arabic system of transliteration. Written Arabic has only a few ways of denoting vowels: three short vowels, three long vowels, and two diphthongs. But written Arabic also rarely shows *any* vowels. South Sudanese vernacular languages have many more vowels and diphthongs than can be or are represented in Arabic script. The transliteration of vernacular names from written Arabic thus distorts the names further. For instance, Renk was named after the nineteenth century Dinka chief Areng (or Arenk) de Chom. In Arabic this is rendered as a definite article and becomes ar-Rang, a perfectly understandable phonetic approximation, but it leaves one wondering who, or what, is "The Rang". Meshra er-Rek is a combination of Arabic mashra' (landing place) and Rek (Rek Dinka), meaning the "Landing Place of the Rek Dinka". But in Arabic it is now written as Mashra' ar-Riqq. So who are the Riqq whose landing place this is supposed to be?

A third layer of confusion has been introduced by NGOs working in Sudan. Some of that confusion is derived from the paucity of vowels in written Arabic. The vowel sound in Ler is pronounced "eh". In Arabic it can be written with a diphthong so that it reads "Lair". But that marking of the diphthong can also be read as a long vowel, pronounced "Leer", and it is as Leer that Ler now appears in NGO reports and on NGO maps. Other mistakes come from mishearing what is said. There are two places named Muot in Lou Nuer country: Muot Dit (Big Muot) and Muot Tot (Little Muot), but the latter regularly appears in NGO reports (even some written by South Sudanese) as Motot. Pul Turuk ("The Pool of the Turks") is now frequently written Pultruk. In many ways NGO mapping, while more accurate than the old Sudan Survey maps in using GPS to locate sites, is even worse than the early twentieth century cartographers in perpetuating garbled or false names.

There is now an opportunity to return to historic names. In the Ingessana Hills, for instance, there are two villages, Bau and Soda, where British officials on trek had their rest houses. As a joke Bau was renamed "Wiska", so that official itineraries read "Wiska and Soda". The name Wiska still appears on some modern maps, but by and large Bau has been reclaimed. Should Meshra er-Rek return to its original name, Meshra Achol, which still appears on some maps as Meshra Ashol? Achol was a nineteenth century Dinka woman who became a prominent trader in her own right. It was at her village that boats landed, it was her landing place. Should Tambura, Arabic for drum, be changed to Tambwa, the praise name of the Zande king after which it is named? Should Deim Zubair, the former headquarters of the most prominent slave-trader in nineteenth century Sudan reclaim its indigenous name of Gbaya (meaning "maize" in Kresh)? And what about South Sudan's rivers? The Bahr el-Jebel (River of the Mountain), Bahr el-Zeraf (River of the Giraffe), and Bahr el-Ghazal (River of the Ghazal) are all internationally recognized names, but each of them lies entirely in South Sudan. South Sudan can name its own rivers if it so chooses.

Some time ago, we had a discussion in the Rift Valley Institute Sudan Course at Rumbek about names used on Sudan maps. Inspired by my St. Louis homie, T.S. Eliot, and his poem, "The Naming of Cats", I composed the following to explain the complexity of Sudanese place maps.

The Naming of (Sudanese) Maps

The Naming of Maps is a difficult matter,
It isn't just one of your holiday games;
You may think at first I'm as mad as a hatter
When I tell you, a map must have THREE DIFFERENT NAMES.
First of all, there's the name that the DCs used daily,
Such as **Wiska** or **Soda**, **Rum-bek**, **Jebelein**,
Such as **Torit** or **Talodi**, or **Wau** or **Opari** –
All of them sensible everyday names.
There are fancier names if you think they sound flasher,
Some for zaribas, some for the deims:
Such as **Nordeng**, **Amadi**, **Genawi**, **El Fasher** –
But all of them sensible everyday names.
But I tell you, a map needs a name that's particular,
A name that's peculiar, and more dignified,
Else how can it keep latitude perpendicular,
Or spread out its landsats, or get in its stride?
Of names of this kind, I can give you a quorum,
Such as **Damazin**, **Yambio**, or **Meshra er-Rek**,

Such as **Mesallamiyya**, or else **Abiemnhom** –
Names that never belong to more than one spec.
But above and beyond there's still one name left over,
And that is the name that you *NEVER* will guess;
The name that no *human research* can discover –
But THE MAP ITSELF KNOWS, and will never confess.
When you notice a map in profound meditation,
The reason, I tell you, is always the same:
Its mind is engaged in a rapt contemplation
Of the thought, of the thought, of the thought of its name:
Its ineffable effable
Cartograffixable
Deep and inscrutable singular Name.

27
RUMBEK AND THE ZARIBAS OF SOUTHERN SUDAN

When visiting Juba once I met a young woman named Nyarek – "Daughter of the Town" in Nuer – so named because she was born in Khartoum, though her parents came from Fangak. But "rek" in Nuer also means "fence". So how did the word for "fence" become the word for "town"? The answer lies in the old zaribas of the nineteenth century.

A zariba is an enclosure. In its simplest form, as used in many parts of the eastern and northern Sudan, it is no more than circle of thorn bushes to keep livestock penned for the night. Armies frequently constructed a zariba as a temporary or semi-permanent camp. The Egyptian and British armies regularly made zaribas of cut thorn bushes surrounding their camps during their nineteenth-century campaigns of conquest in northern Sudan. In the two biggest battles of the Anglo-Egyptian Reconquest of 1898 the Mahdist army at Atbara defended itself within a large oval zariba made from thorn bushes, and the Anglo-Egyptian army at Omdurman similarly protected its firing line with a long line of cut bushes.

A zariba can also be a more permanent fortification, with a ditch or trench dug around it, an earth embankment thrown up above the trench, and sometimes a wooden palisade fixed on top of the surrounding embankment. It was this type of zariba that the ivory- and slave-traders constructed when they established themselves throughout the southern Sudan in the nineteenth century. From the outside these earthworks and palisades looked like a fence. But inside, where the traders and their sailors, soldiers and slaves lived, was a small town, with winding paths between mud huts, and sometimes – especially in the zaribas the Egyptian army later occupied – buildings of brick. So, the fence contained a town, and became a town.

Many of the towns in South Sudan today were first founded as zaribas or have been rebuilt near zaribas sites. Kodok (the old Fashoda) was formerly a zariba, as were Nasir and Bor, Rumbek and Shambe, Wau and Deim Zubeir, Rajaf and Amadi. There are many other abandoned zariba sites throughout Sudan, often recognizable by their ditches, and often marked on the Sudan Survey maps with the name "Khandak" – trench or moat.

The first zariba site I ever saw was at Ayod. Ayod is on a sandy, tree-shaded ridge, with a good supply of clear water from numerous wells. In the 1860s various trading companies established river ports on the Bahr el-Zeraf with a series of inland camps up to Ayod, where they traded in ivory, cattle, slaves. The Ayod zariba was a rectangular trench dug into the sandy ridge. Between Ayod and the river, connecting it to the main river port, was another zariba, which today still goes by the name "Khandak". These zaribas were in operation for only about a decade. In 1875, when Gordon was acting as governor-general of Equatoria, he closed down the camps and evacuated the traders who manned them. Ironically, he decided to employ one of these traders – a Danaqla named Nasir Ali – and sent him up the Sobat to establish a new government station. It was located at a spot called "Noor" – palm tree – by the Nuer, from the palm trees planted there. To the rest of the world it became known after the man who founded it – Nasir. Present-day Nasir town is now located across the river from the original zariba (see chapter 28).

Both Ayod and Nasir were small compared to Pendit (Dinka for "Big Town") located near present-day Rumbek. This was the very first camp in what became an extended commercial ivory- and slave-trading network that exploited South Sudan throughout the middle of the nineteenth century. Alphonse de Malzac, a French diplomat turned hunter and trader, was the first to break out of the restrictions the Egyptian government had imposed on ivory-traders working along the Bahr el-Jebel. From a base at the river port of Shambe, he created a network of strategic alliances with the Cic and Agar Dinka in 1854-6, founding his first zariba among the Dinka Agar. De Malzac exploited tribal feuds and inter-tribal wars to penetrate the interior and expand his trading network. Using musket-armed Arab Sudanese retainers as the backbone of his military force, he allied with specific groups of Dinka against their local enemies. Cattle taken in these raids were used to feed his own troops, reward his allies, and trade for ivory. Captives taken in these raids were given to his retainers as slaves. Thus the connection between ivory-trading and slave-raiding was forged.

De Malzac established the first set of rules for the internal administration of zaribas. These were adopted by later commercial companies for running their zaribas and became known in Arabic as the "kanun Malzac" (Malzac's laws). He did not live long to enjoy his commercial success, dying in 1860 after a long illness in Khartoum, "fortified by the Sacraments of the Latin Church" (so it was later reported). The zariba system he establsihed, which has since been associated with such famous northern Sudanese Arab slave-merchants as Zubair Pasha, was thus initiated by European traders, and assisted by local South Sudanese allies.

The zaribas varied in size, according to whether they were temporary way-stations along a caravan route, or small outpost, or long-term permanent settlement. The smallest contained no more than about twenty huts, but by the late 1860s the average sized zariba had about 250 armed men, plus their women, children and slaves. In 1870 the Austrian explorer Georg Schweinfurth estimated that the total immigrant population in the zaribas of the twelve great Khartoum trading companies in the Bahr al-Ghazal amounted to about 10,000 men: soldiers, merchants, clerks, holy men, and other adventurers. In addition to this the camps included a total of 5-11,000 slave soldiers, 40-60,000 personal slaves, and about 190,000 subject population settled around the camps and along the caravan routes, who were neither slave nor fully free, and were employed as porters, labourers, and agricultural workers. They were towns, indeed.

Rumbek became a government station in the 1870s when the Italian soldier of fortune and ex-Garibaldini, Romolo Gessi, used it as his base to defeat the revolt of the *jallaba* in Bahr el-Ghazal, led by Zubair Pasha's son, Sulaiman Zubair. Rumbek became one of Egypt's main commercial and military outposts in the South. At the beginning of the Mahdiya the Egyptian garrison at Rumbek was slaughtered in July 1883 by a combined force of Dinka and Nuer. The official version of this defeat (reported by Emin Pasha) was that the garrison was caught outside the zariba when on an unauthorized raid against the Dinka Agar. Another government official claimed that the Dinka attack on Rumbek was led "by a great sorcerer" chanting "the deadly invocation of the Arab" then being heard throughout Sudan as the Mahdist revolt grew in strength. In fact the assault on Rumbek had nothing to do with the inspiration of Mahdism. The Dinka and Nuer versions of the raid revolve around the personality of the famous (or notorious) Dinka Agar leader Wol Athiaan.

Wol had dealings with the Egyptian garrison, as his sister was the wife of the Egyptian commander there. According to the Nuer, it was the Egyptians who made Wol a chief of the Agar. He therefore had inside knowledge of the zariba's strengths, weaknesses, and the activities of the "Turuk", as the Dinka and Nuer called the Egyptians and other outsiders from the north. As the successes of the Mahdi elsewhere in Sudan grew throughout 1882 and 1883 he enlisted the Agar's erstwhile enemies, the Nyuong, Dok and Jagei Nuer. Prior to launching the assault on the zariba, however, he gave separate instructions to the Agar warriors: they were to wear a strip of white cloth around their arm or body to distinguish them from their Nuer allies. Then, he said, "As you spear the Turuk to your right, spear the Nuer to your left". The assault was successful, the Egyptian garrison was wiped out, but either during or after the battle (the Nuer say after) the Agar turned on the Nuer, trying to rid themselves of two enemies at once. The resulting feud was to disturb Nuer-Dinka relations well into the twentieth century.

When the Anglo-Egyptian forces arrived in Bahr al-Ghazal at the beginning of the twentieth century they reoccupied the Rumbek area and established the current town at some distance from the old zariba site. Wol Athiaan continued an ambivalent relationship with both the new government and his Nuer neighbours, alternately collaborating and fighting with them both. The government temporarily exiled him to Wau in 1921 and allowed him to return to the vicinity of Rumbek in 1922. He died in 1948, his death marked, so local people say, by a meteorite shower.

The events of the nineteenth century are still remembered. A village has grown up around the zariba site of Pendit, but the site itself remains mainly unoccupied. In 2006 I asked some young men of the village why this was so, and they replied, "We are still angry".

Further reading:
>   Richard Gray, *The Southern Sudan, 1839-1889*
>   Paul Lane and Douglas H. Johnson, "The archaeology and history of slavery in South Sudan in the nineteenth century", in Andrew Peacock (ed.) *The Frontiers of the Ottoman World*

28
PAST STATES 1: "GREATER" UPPER NILE

People in South Sudan still often refer to the territories of "Greater Upper Nile", "Greater Bahr el-Ghazal" and "Greater Equatoria", collectively known as "The Greaters". These were the three southern provinces at Sudan's independence in 1956 and when the Southern Region was established in 1972. They were reconstituted as regions when the Southern Region was abolished in 1983, before being redivided into the current ten states of South Sudan. But how did these territories come into existence, and have they always contained the same peoples and districts? I start here with Upper Nile, the oldest territory, the one which has undergone the most name changes and boundary adjustments, and the one from which the other two provinces emerged.

What is now known as Greater Upper Nile was constructed from territories along the White Nile and Bahr el-Jebel. Before the Turco-Egyptian conquest the White Nile was dominated by the Shilluk and Dinka. The royal capital of the Shilluk kingdom was inland at Pacodo ("the village of the hornless cattle"), now often written as Fashoda. The Shilluk raided as far north as Abba Island (on which they even had a settlement). The Dinka communities were spread along the east bank of the river from just south of Jebelein to the Sobat and were often in conflict with the Sennar sultanate on the Blue Nile. It was only after Egyptian flotillas had penetrated the *sudd* blockage on the Bahr el-Jebel as far as Gondokoro in 1839-41 that the Turco-Egyptian government based in Khartoum attempted to administer this region directly.

White Nile was first made a district in 1855 when a governor was sent to garrison a fort at the Sobat mouth, but White Nile district was amalgamated with Sennar and Khartoum provinces in 1856 and the Sobat garrison was withdrawn in 1857. The town of Kaka became the main settlement for traders from

Dongola and by 1860 they so threatened the position of the Shilluk *reth* that he expelled them from the area. But in 1861 one of the freebooters, Muhammad Khair, re-established himself at Kaka with an army of 1000 riflemen and 200 Baggara allies, drove the *reth* from his capital and controlled the Shilluk territory on the west bank of the White Nile. The *reth* urged the Egyptian authorities to intervene and in 1863 the Egyptian army ousted Muhammad Khair from Kaka. It was at this time that White Nile was now made a province with its capital at the river port of Fashoda.

Throughout the 1870s the territory now called Greater Upper Nile was shared between two or three other provinces. In 1870 the Khedive Ismail sent the British explorer, Sir Samuel Baker, to found a new province of Equatoria. On his first attempt Baker could not get past the sudd on the Bahr el-Jebel so returned to the White Nile and founded the garrison of Taufikia, south of present day Malakal, where he camped before his second, and successful journey south. In 1871 Ismail merged Khartoum, Sennar and White Nile into a single province called Southern Sudan, but restored the three provinces the next year. In the meantime various river stations, little more than landing stages, came under the jurisdiction of the governor of Equatoria: Hillet Nuer (now Adok), Shambe, and Bor on the Bahr el-Jebel, and Nasir on the Sobat.

The founding of Nasir is a curious story. In 1874 Colonel Charles George Gordon succeeded Baker as governor of Equatoria. He cleared out the ivory and slave-trading camps along the Bahr el-Zeraf, but employed their leader, Nasir Ali, along with 100 ex-slavers to set up a camp 100 miles up the Sobat to intercept slave raiding expeditions coming from Fadassi on the Blue Nile. The original site of Nasir town was on the left bank of the river, at a place called Noor, so called because of its palm trees (Noor in Nuer). So the slavers became anti-slavery police, but raided the locale so extensively that the surrounding Nuer and Anyuak villages were deserted by the end of the century.

The river port of Fashoda remained a province capital under both the Egyptians and Mahdists throughout the 1880s and 1890s, and it was Fashoda that the French under Captain Marchand occupied in 1898, in their bid to create an empire stretching from Senegal's Atlantic coast in the west to the border with Ethiopia in the east. When Kitchener arrived with his own force he established a camp near Fashoda and sent troops to re-occupy Taufikia and Nasir. Fashoda town was reoccupied after the French withdrew.

It is from this point that the administrative history of Upper Nile Province really begins. Fashoda District, including the White Nile valley south of Abba Island, the Sobat and the Bahr el-Ghazal, was gazetted on 29 December 1898. Bahr el-Ghazal was reoccupied and separated from Fashoda in 1901, and in 1903 Fashoda District became Upper Nile Province, with Fashoda town renamed Kodok, and the Shilluk royal capital alone retaining the name in its original form of Pachodo. In 1905 the province's northern boundary was fixed at Jebelein, including the Seleim Baggara, and the southern boundary extended all the way to Uganda, including Mongalla District. In 1906 Mongalla was separated from Upper Nile, and in 1917 Jebelain and the Seleim Baggara were transferred to White Nile Province.

During the first two decades of the twentieth centuries many of the towns and outposts now associated with Upper Nile were founded. A police post was established at Renk (named after the Dinka chief Areng de Chum) in 1901. Abwong was founded for the Inspector of the Sobat Valley in 1904, and a customs and trading post at Gambela on the Baro River was leased from the Ethiopian government (it was never part of Sudan). Both Bor and Mongalla were created by 1905, and forts were built at Akobo and Pibor Post in 1912 as part of military operations against the Anyuak and Murle. In 1914 the province capital was transferred to the newly built town of Malakal and Taufikia was abandoned. By 1915 the main district headquarters were at Renk, Melut, Kodok, Tonga, Malakal, Abwong and Nasir. Nasir, in fact, was peripatetic, the military and civil headquarters exchanging sites across the river with each other until the town was finally anchored on its present site and Noor was abandoned altogether in 1925.

There were numerous district transfers and boundary changes with neighbouring Mongalla, Bahr el-Ghazal, Kordofan and Blue Nile provinces, the most frequent being with Mongalla. In 1910 the boundary between the two provinces was fixed along the Nuer-Dinka boundary, and in 1926 the Dinka of Duk Faweil, Jonglei, and Kongor were transferred to Upper Nile while Bor and Aliab were transferred to Bahr el-Ghazal. But in 1928 Bor was transferred to Upper Nile while the Aliab were absorbed into Yirol District, which was also transferred to Upper Nile. The Eastern District, Bahr el-Ghazal, containing the western Nuer and some Rueng Dinka, also became part of Upper Nile in 1929 (and continued to be known locally as "Eastern District, Bahr el-Ghazal" for many years). Yirol District was transferred to the new Equatorial Province (made by combining Mongalla and Bahr el-Ghazal) in 1936.

A Nuba Mountains Province had been created by detaching Dilling, Kadugli, Tegale and Talodi from Kordofan in 1913. In 1923 Kaka town was transferred to Nuba Mountains, as were Tonga town and Morada in 1927, but not the surrounding countryside in each case. The Rueng Dinka of Eastern District, Bahr el-Ghazal were transferred to Talodi in 1928. When the Nuba Mountains Province was re-amalgamated with Kordofan Province in 1929 Tonga, Morada and Kaka reverted to Upper Nile, and the Rueng were re-incorporated into the Western Nuer District in 1931.

By 1936 the outline of Upper Nile Province was pretty much what it would become in 1956, except for its border with Blue Nile Province. In 1925 the Burun settlements along the Daga River had been transferred from Blue Nile (then Fung Province) to Upper Nile, and in 1938 the Koma and Uduk of Yabus and Chali el-Fil joined them, the Mabaan and Uduk being administered from Renk, while the Koma were administered from Nasir. Yet in 1953 the Koma and Uduk were returned to Blue Nile, it being thought that it would be easier to administer them from Kurmuk. Thus was created an anomaly, a group of peoples with strong affinities with their southern neighbours being excluded from South Sudan because the date of their transfer preceded independence by two and a half years (see chapter 34).

With Sudan's independence on 1 January 1956 the lease on Gambela expired and the enclave reverted to Ethiopia.

The outline and content of Upper Nile were created along lines of communication (mainly the rivers), and on security considerations of pacification and placing rival communities under a single administrative jurisdiction. Districts which are now claimed by Greater Equatoria and Greater Bahr el-Ghazal (and even Kordofan, White Nile, and Blue Nile) were once part of Upper Nile. The challenge now is how to maintain these older social ties across new administrative boundaries.

Further reading:
    Richard Gray, *The Southern Sudan, 1839-1889*
    Richard L. Hill, *Egypt in the Sudan 1820-1881*
    C.A. Willis, et al., *The Upper Nile Province Handbook: a report on peoples and government in the southern Sudan, 1931*

29
PAST STATES 2: "GREATER" BAHR EL-GHAZAL

Bahr el-Ghazal is the second oldest province, but with the oldest name of the three. Before the nineteenth century the communities living along the Bahr el-Arab/Kiir river were the only people who had regular contact with the states and peoples of the north. The Darfur sultanate regularly raided into western Bahr el-Ghazal, the Hofrat en-Nahas–Kafia Kingi–Raga area then known as Dar Fartit. But many of the Arab cattle keepers, such as the Rizeigat and the Misseriya, periodically sought refuge with the peoples south of the Bahr el-Arab/Kiir, particularly the Dinka, when trying to escape taxation and other demands of the Darfur sultan. All this changed in the nineteenth century when Bahr el-Ghazal was dominated by new trade patterns introduced through the zariba system.

Trade, principally for ivory, was confined mainly to the Bahr el-Jebel until 1854 when the French diplomat and trader Alphonse de Malzac established a river port at Ghaba Shambil (now Shambe) among the Dinka Cic. From here he set off on trading expeditions into the interior and founded the first inland zariba – fortified trading centre – near present day Rumbek. Rumbek became an important trading hub with caravan tracks leading southwest towards the Zande kingdoms and northwest towards Darfur (chapter 27).

But Bahr el-Ghazal was to be opened up to commerce by a more direct river route. In 1855 boats belonging to the British trader and consul John Petherick discovered the mouth of the Bahr el-Ghazal feeding into Lake No where it joins the Bahr el-Jebel to form the White Nile. By 1856 boats were landing at the lagoon that later became known as Meshra er-Rek and this became the main starting point for the network of caravan tracks and zaribas that soon covered the interior of Bahr el-Ghazal.

Also in 1856 there arrived Zubair Rahma Mansur, a man who was soon to dominate the Bahr el-Ghazal trade. Ten years later he made an alliance with the Rizeigat of southern Darfur and so secured the routes to Kordofan and Darfur. By 1869 there were more than eighty zaribas between the river Rohl near Rumbek and the river Lol, the lengthy western tributary of the Bahr el-Arab/Kiir. Zaribas were sited every fifteen to eighteen miles between the Dinka and Azande country. The most important trading centre was Deim Zubair, Zubair Rahma Mansur's capital, with its link to the Zande kingdoms in the south and Darfur in the north. Zubair was so powerful that after he fought, defeated and killed the Egyptian governor sent to take control of the province, Egypt had no choice but to recognize him as governor of Bahr el-Ghazal in 1873.

Zubair launched his conquest of Darfur from Deim Zubair in 1874, but this time he overreached himself. Going to Cairo to confirm his claim he was detained and had to leave his trading empire in the hands of his less able son, Sulaiman, who in 1878-9 revolted against Egyptian rule, was defeated and executed. The zariba network, including Rumbek (then part of Equatoria Province), Wau, and Deim Zubair, was now under Egyptian control, and it was from there that the new governor, the Italian adventurer Romolo Gessi, expanded Egyptian influence to include many of the Zande kingdoms. The most famous of the Zande kings, Yambio (or Gbudwe) was captured and briefly imprisoned in Wau until released by the invading Mahdist forces in 1885.

While the Ansar (Mahdists) invaded northern Bahr el-Ghazal from Kordofan and Darfur, a series of Dinka revolts erupted throughout the province, the most successful being led by the resourceful Dinka leader Wol Athiaan who destroyed the garrison at Rumbek. But though the province fell to the Ansar it was abandoned after the death of the Mahdi in 1885. Throughout the 1890s the peoples of Bahr el-Ghazal had to contend with a number of brief raids from Ansar garrisons in the north and Equatoria, as well as Rizeigat from Darfur. The Belgian advance from the Congo into Zandeland and Equatoria in the late 1890s put an end to the local Ansar threat. But it was the French invasion of 1898 that embroiled Bahr el-Ghazal briefly in the territorial rivalries of imperial powers. Captain Marchand first contracted an alliance with the Zande king Tembura, and then made Wau the base from which he advanced on Fashoda. The foundations of the French Fort Desaix still can be seen incorporated in the Wau Town Council building today.

After the French were forced to evacuate their posts in Sudan in 1898 Bahr el-Ghazal was declared part of Fashoda District. In 1901 Bahr el-Ghazal was reoccupied by the Egyptian army, Wau became the province capital and military headquarters, Rumbek, Shambe and other stations were revived. The province was transferred from military to Sudan government authority at the beginning of 1902. The Zande kingdoms were incorporated into the province by 1905, when King Gbudwe was defeated and killed by an Egyptian army force from Wau and is buried in what is now Yambio town.

The boundary with Kordofan and Darfur was subject to several negotiations. In 1905 the Ngok and Twic Dinka were transferred from Bahr el-Ghazal to Kordofan Province, but while the Ngok remained in Kordofan the Twic were later reabsorbed into Bahr el-Ghazal. In 1912 a local agreement set the boundary between Darfur and Bahr el-Ghazal at the Bahr el-Arab/Kiir, recognizing the territory south of the river as belonging to the Malual Dinka. But this was overturned in 1918 by the British governor of the newly conquered Darfur Province, when he declared the boundary to be forty miles south of the river, giving all of that territory to the Rizeigat, who had helped the British overthrow sultan Ali Dinar in 1916. The Dinka naturally resisted this land grab and after the Arianhdit rising of 1921 the Sudan government re-examined the issue, setting a new boundary fourteen miles south of the river in the Wheatley-

Munro agreement of 1924. The Malual have disputed this boundary ever since (see chapter 32).

The eastern part of the province underwent a number of changes in the 1920s and 1930s. Though nominally under Bahr el-Ghazal jurisdiction no attempt was made to administer the western Nuer until 1922 when the District Commissioner of Rumbek first visited the Nyuong Nuer. Various other groups were then added to the Eastern District: the Aliab Dinka in 1925, followed by Bor (as the administrative headquarters for the Aliab) in 1926, then the Nuer and Dinka of Nuba Mountains Province early in 1927, and the Ruweng Dinka from Dar Homr District in Kordofan the same year. Bor was retransferred to Upper Nile Province in 1928, while at the same time the Aliab were added to Yirol District, which was then transferred to Upper Nile. The Eastern District (western Nuer and Ruweng (Panriang) Dinka) was finally transferred to Upper Nile in 1929, placing all the Nuer under one provincial authority.

In 1936, partly as a cost-cutting exercise, and partly in preparation for creating a single southern province, Bahr el-Ghazal and Mongalla were amalgamated as Equatorial Province with its capital at Juba, and a sub-provincial capital at Wau. Yirol District was transferred from Upper Nile to become part of the new province. This arrangement lasted until 1948 when Bahr el-Ghazal once again became a separate province consisting of Aweil, Western (Raga), Jur River (Tonj) and Lakes (Rumbek) Districts, the Zande districts of Tembura and Yambio being retained by Equatoria. Bahr el-Ghazal had now attained its final outline, except for the Western District.

The area of Hofrat en-Nahas and Kafia Kingi in Western District bordered on Darfur and many Darfur peoples had crossed into it (Stanislaus Paysama was brought here when he was freed from slavery). When the Southern Policy was announced in 1930 the governor of Bahr el-Ghazal expelled the provinces by burning the evacuated villages and closing the station at Kafia Kingi (chapter 1). After independence Hofrat en-Nahas and Kafia Kingi were annexed to Darfur in 1960. Because the Addis Ababa Agreement of 1972 defined the Southern Region according to its 1956 boundaries this territory was supposed to be returned to the administration of Bahr el-Ghazal, but President Nimeiri instructed the governor of Darfur to delay its return. The area is still occupied by Southern Darfur State, despite the terms of the Comprehensive Peace Agreement that confirm the boundaries previously defined in the Addis Ababa Agreement (see chapter 33).

Further reading:
Richard Gray, *The Southern Sudan, 1839-1889*
Robert O. Collins, *Shadows in the Grass: Britain in the southern Sudan, 1918-1956*
Douglas H. Johnson, *When Boundaries become Borders: the impact of boundary-making in southern Sudan's frontier zones*

30
PAST STATES 3: "GREATER" EQUATORIA

Equatoria was the most elastic province, a region including districts that used to belong to the other two. The very name is elusive, first appearing in the nineteenth century, then disappearing completely, then being revived under two different permutations in the twentieth century.

When an Egyptian flotilla found a way through the *sudd* in 1839-40 the Bahr el-Jebel was opened up to both official and private commerce, at least as far as Gondokoro, on the east bank of the river. But it wasn't until 1870 that Khedive Ismail of Egypt initiated formal control over the region when he appointed the British explorer, Sir Samuel Baker, the first governor of a new province of Equatoria, separate from the rest of Sudan. Baker reached Gondokoro in 1871, formally announced its annexation to Egypt, and attempted to expand Egypt's empire into the Great Lakes region of modern-day Uganda.

Baker's governorship was not a great success. Sent to suppress the slave-trade, he only succeeded in preying upon the Bari, whom he was supposed to protect, and antagonizing the kingdom of Bunyoro, which he tried to annex. His successor, Charles Gordon, paired back these ambitions. He focused on securing the communications along the Bahr el-Jebel by establishing two new stations at Lado and Rejaf in 1874, moving the province headquarters from Gondokoro to Lado, and, in 1879 (by which time he was governor-general of all of Sudan), withdrawing all the garrisons along the Victoria Nile for lack of money. "Equatoria" in Gordon's day included the Bahr el-Jebel from the Sobat mouth to Wadelai (now in Uganda), the Sobat river as far as Nasir, the district of Rohl (Rumbek), and caravan routes radiating both east and west from the river stations. Amadi, an important commercial, administrative, and military centre, was one of the westernmost outposts of the province.

Gordon's eventual successor was the German medical doctor Eduard Schnitzer, better known as Emin Bey (later Emin Pasha). It was Emin's fate to have to confront the Mahdist invasion of South Sudan in the 1880s. But after the fall of Bahr el-Ghazal Province Mahidst forces got no further than Amadi, which they captured in 1885, before withdrawing north following the Mahdi's death after the fall of Khartoum. Emin had a respite until 1888 when a new invasion force arrived. Finding Lado abandoned it advanced on and took the Rejaf garrison. The remaining Egyptian force – mainly South Sudanese soldiers – held out in Dufile and Wadelai until 1889, when Emin was "rescued" by Henry Morton Stanley and escorted to Zanzibar, leaving substantial garrisons of southern Sudanese troops at Wadelai and Kavalli's in Uganda. These soldiers became the ancestors of East Africa's "Nubi" communities (chapter 23).

For some time these independent garrisons held off the Mahdist forces, which were split between Bor and Rejaf, using the latter base to send raiding parties east and west. Aside from these garrisons the rest of former Equatoria was free of occupation. But in 1897 a new power arrived in the region with forces employed by the Belgian King Leopold's Congo Free State. In two battles at Bedden and Rejaf they defeated the remaining Mahdist garrison, who withdrew to Bor. In 1898, following the defeat of the Khalifa Abdallhi at Omdurman, the last Mahdist army retreated out of Equatoria and South Sudan.

At the end of 1898, then, there was no longer an "Equatoria". The Belgian Congo occupied the Lado Enclave, which included the west bank of the river extending north of Lado, while Uganda (under British control) administered the posts at Nimule and Gondokoro. Only part of present-day Mundari country was included in the territory claimed and occupied by the Anglo-Egyptian Sudan.

The new Sudan government aimed to restrict Belgian activities to its enclave, the personal property of King Leopold, which was set to revert to Sudan on his death. A post was established at Mongalla in 1900 to watch the Belgians, and a river port was re-established at Bor in 1905. Maridi was divided between the Belgians camped on the site of the present town, and an Anglo-Egyptian garrison from Bahr el-Ghazal camped at "old Maridi" a few miles north.

In 1906 Mongalla Province was separated from Upper Nile Province. It contained only two districts: Bor and Mongalla, with Mongalla the province capital. It expanded slowly: in 1908 Aliab District was formed and then added to Bor, and the Kongor police post was founded. In 1909 Kongor and Duk Faiwel were added to Bor District, another post was created at Duk Fadiat in 1910, and the border between Mongalla and Upper Nile Provinces was settled at the Dinka-Nuer boundary north of the two Duks. Despite this tribal-provincial demarcation, when an administrative post was established at Ayod among the Gaawar Nuer in 1917 it came under the jurisdiction of Mongalla, and remained so until 1921.

In 1910 King Leopold died and the Lado Enclave was absorbed into Mongalla Province, adding Yei and Rejaf-Kajo Kaji districts (which at the time extended as far south as Lake Albert). The Belgians left behind five cemeteries, whose remains can still be seen: at Lado, Rejaf, Kiro, Yei and Loka. From this time on Mongalla also began to expand both west and east.

In 1913 the headquarters of Aliab District was moved to Tombe, and Amadi District was formed as the western-most district. The frontier with Uganda was adjusted so that Sudan took over the Bari and Latuka country east of the Bahr el-Jebel while ceding the Madi and Lugbara south of Kajo Kaji to Uganda. Torit was founded in 1914, and the Didinga around Nagishot were taken over from Uganda in 1923. Madial and Tseretenya were taken over from Uganda in 1926, Maridi District was transferred from Bahr el-Ghazal to Mongalla in 1927, and in that same year Sudan occupied Toposa country in the far east, moving the Eastern District headquarters from Nagishot to Kapoeta.

While Mongalla expanded east, west, and to a certain extent south, its northern boundary contracted. In 1926 the Dinka-Nuer District containing Duk Faiwel, Jonglei and Kongor was transferred to Upper Nile Province, and Aliab District (with Bor as its headquarters) was transferred to Bahr el-Ghazal.

The early 1930s saw some internal reorganization. The Central District was formed in 1929 by amalgamating Mongalla and Rejaf Districts. The province headquarters was moved to Juba in 1930, while the military headquarters of the Equatorial Corps was moved to Torit. In 1931 Yambio and Tembura Districts of Bahr el-Ghazal were amalgamated and Maridi District was divided, with the Azande being absorbed into Yambio District and the Moru, Avukaya and Baka being placed under the jurisdiction of Amadi. In 1935 Opari-Kajo Kaji District was abolished with Kajo Kaji being absorbed into Yei District and Opari amalgamated with Latuka. Yambio District (now including all Azande) was transferred to Mongalla, becoming Zande District.

By 1935, then, Mongalla Province included all the districts that are now considered part of "Greater Equatoria": Central District (Juba, Mongalla, Rejaf), Yei River District (Yei, Kajo Kaji), Moru District (Amadi, Terakeka, Maridi), Latuka District (Torit, Opari), Eastern District (Nagishot, Kapoeta), and Zande District (Yambio, Tembura).

Then in 1936 Mongalla and Bahr el-Ghazal provinces, along with Yirol District of Upper Nile, were incorporated to form one super province, called Equatorial Province, with Juba as its province headquarters. The name Equatoria was finally making a comeback, although in a different form.

This did not last, however, and in 1948 the two provinces were once again separated, with Mongalla Province in its 1935 territory now emerging as Equatoria Province, again with Juba as its headquarters.

So, what can we learn from this recital of the history of the three "Greater" regions of South Sudan? It might surprise some to learn that originally, and for a very long time, not only Bor and Kongor, but their Nuer neighbours as well, belonged to what we now call Equatoria. The Azande were considered part of Bahr el-Ghazal from the nineteenth century until the mid-1930s. Bits of Bahr el-Ghazal and Upper Nile belonged to the Nuba Mountains, parts of Bahr el-Ghazal have been annexed by Darfur, and slices of Upper Nile passed back and forth between it and Kordofan and Blue Nile. Even internal districts, which some might believe have "always" existed, were reshaped and refashioned as the provinces expanded and contracted into the outlines they assumed at the time of Sudan's independence. Boundary making is always a delicate business, constantly being re-drawn, and rarely completely finished.

Note: The "old" spellings of some place names have been retained, but deciding how to spell names on a map, like demarcation, can be a never-ending business.

Further reading:
  Richard Gray, *The Southern Sudan, 1839-1889*
  Robert O. Collins, *Shadows in the Grass: Britain in the southern Sudan, 1918-1956*

31
WHAT WAS THE PURPOSE OF THE JONGLEI CANAL?

Egypt, as is commonly said, is the gift of the Nile. After Britain helped Egypt re-conquer Sudan in 1898, and after the signing of the Anglo-Egyptian Agreement in 1899, the Nile came under British control from its source in Lake Victoria to its mouth on the Mediterranean. Egypt had the opportunity for the first time in its history of regulating the entire length of the river. In 1904 the British head of the Egyptian Irrigation Department, Sir William Garstin travelled to Sudan to investigate the possibility of increasing and regulating the flow of the Nile waters. On his return to Egypt he proposed an ambitious plan of building dams in Uganda and Sudan to create new reservoirs where water could be stored and released in years of a low river. There was one main obstacle to releasing the increased upstream flow to Egypt downstream: the *sudd*.

The *sudd* (Arabic for a dam or obstruction) in what is now Jonglei State is a vast papyrus swamp. It has sometimes been likened to a great sponge soaking up the water that flows into it. Water is dispersed out of the main channel into the surrounding swamp where a great deal of water is released into the atmosphere by transpiration from the leaves of the packed vegetation. There was little point to increasing the water flowing *into* the swamp if there was no guarantee that would increase the water flowing *out* of the swamp. Garstin's solution was to propose a '*sudd* diversion channel' to route the water to the east of the swamp, either joining up with the Pibor-Sobat river system that flowed back into the Nile, or rejoining the Nile above the Sobat mouth.

The exact route of this diversion channel remained undecided while various surveys were undertaken. Finally, shortly before World War II broke out it was announced that the canal would run from near the village of Jonglei to the White Nile before it joined the Sobat, and it was from this hypothetical starting point that the canal got its name.

The line on the map might have made hydrological sense to those in Cairo and Khartoum who drew it, but it didn't make sense to one person. John Winder ("Tokrial", as he was known to the Nuer) was the District Commissioner at Fangak. He spoke Nuer and had walked all over his district. He wrote a letter to Khartoum pointing out that the proposed route of the canal would block the flow of water from a series of khors into the main river and interfere with seasonal cattle migrations. As he explained to me many years later, "I didn't know if all this would happen, but I knew no one in Khartoum had thought about it."

The outbreak of the war but a halt to this ambitious development scheme, but Winder's letter meant that the Jonglei canal portion of the plan could not go ahead until a thorough environmental study of the area was made. Winder himself was appointed to the first Jonglei Investigation Team in the late 1940s, and he was the governor of Upper Nile Province when the second team completed its report in 1954. This multi-volume report documented the hydrology, livelihoods, livestock management and agriculture of an area stretching from around Mongalla to Kosti, assessing the impact the canal would have on the inhabitants of the region in order to plan better how to ameliorate that impact.

By this time, however, parts of Garstin's grand scheme had come under attack in Uganda, where the Ugandan government decided that it did not want to build a dam at the outlet of Lake Albert, raising the lake level and flooding the surrounding countryside, just to give Egypt more water. Thus one of the main justifications for the canal – that of speeding an increased flow from Uganda northwards – had been eliminated.

The Jonglei Project was shelved temporarily for various reasons, insecurity in the area throughout the 1960s being not the least of them. One of the criticisms levelled at the Khartoum government by a succession of exile South Sudanese movements was that Khartoum had deliberately kept the South underdeveloped by abandoning the canal scheme, but there were others who were not so sure. By the time the civil war ended in 1972 the 1958 Nile Waters Agreement had changed the hydropolitics of the Nile by defining the upper limits of the Nile waters to be shared out between Egypt and Sudan. Sudan now had plans to increase cultivation massively in order to become the "bread basket" of the Middle East, but for either country to increase the amount of water it used, the total amount of water flowing through the Nile had to be increased. Since Uganda still was not interested in flooding a large part of its territory to satisfy Egypt and Sudan's water needs, that meant that a new source of water had to be found. This required either squeezing the water out of the great sponge of the *sudd* swamp, or diverting water away from the *sudd*. Thus the Jonglei Canal project was reborn.

With a Southern Regional Government newly installed, however, the construction of the canal could not be ordered by Khartoum just like that. It had to be sold to politicians and people alike. In the mid 1960s the level of Lake Victoria in East Africa had risen dramatically, causing high floods and the expansion of the swamp in much of the Jonglei area. The swamp had not receded even after the lake levels dropped. The canal, it was now alleged, would be a flood control mechanism, reducing the area of the swamp back to its 1950s area, providing a new all-season road paralleling the canal, bringing new water sources to the inland areas, and providing an area for the expansion of irrigated and mechanised farming.

That was the publicity. The Southern Region's politicians were soon made aware that support for the canal was required if they were to continue to have a political career: leaders who publicly opposed the canal were either arrested or driven, temporarily, into exile. The canal's new plan had a number of critics. International environmentalists were worried what the proposed drainage of the *sudd* would do to the region's eco-system. But local people had more immediate concerns. The canal line crossed many seasonal grazing routes where pastoralists brought their cattle to the edge of the swamp for dry season grazing. How would the reduction of the swamp affect the distribution of grasses? How would the canal itself affect the drainage of water after the rainy season?

New research teams were sent out, with the socio-economic research carried out independently from the environmental research, though the two were interconnected. People were told that a number of crossing points (fords or bridges) would be spaced along the canal for cattle to cross, that pipes would be laid as water points while the canal was dug so that water could be drawn off for local use. A brief alteration to the canal line was made, so that it no longer ended at Jonglei (now surrounded by water), but would be diverted to the east of Bor before rejoining the river south of Bor. A great bucket-wheel digging machine was brought from Pakistan to gauge out the new canal line starting near the Sobat mouth, simultaneously building an embankment along the eastern flank of the canal on top of which the new road would run.

In the end none of these promises were kept. Water pipes were not laid beneath the road as promised, raising questions as to whether there was any intention of allowing water to be drawn off for local use. The proposed cattle crossing points were reduced, and the bridges abandoned entirely, meaning that cattle would have to congregate at fewer points in order swim across the canal. A road embankment was raised, but it was not packed down firmly enough so that it soon was subject to erosion and deterioration. And because water from the eastern plains could no longer drain towards the swamp, but backed up along the road embankment, inland areas began to suffer from a new pattern of flooding.

In truth the canal was being constructed in the cheapest way possible and designed to bring water north, not share it for local development. Its very alignment minimized the advantages it might have brought to local communities and increased the disadvantages. Had it been aligned further east – passing between Ayod and Waat, separating the Gaawar and Lou Nuer – it would have been less disruptive to season grazing patterns. It also could have brought water closer to the eastern plains, which are desperately dry during the rainy season. But none of this was done.

The canal was halted by the outbreak of war. The ditch reached an area near Panyagoor in what is now Twic East County. There the bucket machine stopped, and there it remains. It is difficult to see how the project can be revived to bring some benefit to the communities it has already damaged. This would require filling it in and starting all over again.

Further reading:
>Robert O. Collins, *The Waters of the Nile: hydropolitics and the Jonglei Canal 1900-1988*
>Paul Howell, Mike Lock & Stephen Cobb (eds), *The Jonglei Canal: impact and opportunity*

32
WHAT WAS
THE WHEATLEY-MUNRO AGREEMENT?

A short time ago someone working on Sudan's border issues asked me if I knew anything about a "Whitley-Monroe Agreement", which was alleged to pertain "in some way" to the alignment of the Northern Bahr el Ghazal/South Darfur border. The request illustrated two facts about South Sudan's history: 1) the long reach of past events into the present, and 2) how quickly that history is lost on the official consciousness. The Wheatley-Munro Agreement was supposed to settle an old boundary dispute between the Dinka Malual, known to Dinka people as Malual-Giernyang, and the Rizeigat Baggara, but it has, itself, become a new line of disagreement. It was inextricably bound up in the shifting political alliances of imperial conquest.

When the Anglo-Egyptian army began the reoccupation of Bahr el-Ghazal in 1901 the neighbouring sultanate of Darfur was still an independent state. The boundary between Darfur and the Anglo-Egyptian province of Bahr el-Ghazal was then recognized as the Bahr el-Arab/Kiir, though it was some years before authorities in either Khartoum or Wau knew exactly where that river ran: it was known by different names at different sections along its lenth. But one thing they were sure of was that the Dinka south of the river had successfully defended their territory from invaders from Darfur. A handbook of Bahr el-Ghazal Province published in 1911 recorded that the Dinka had repelled "irruptions" by "the Rizeigat and other Arabs from Darfur" three times during the end of the nineteenth century and had defeated an invading Mahdist army from Darfur in 1893.

Rizeigat raiding parties continued to cross into Bahr el-Ghazal during the first decade of the twentieth century, and in 1912 a border settlement between the Rizeigat and Malual was finally brokered by the local British inspector. The settlement was agreed between the two most powerful border leaders, sultan Musa Madibbo of the Rizeigat and chief Awutiek of the Malual (known to the Arabs and British as Chak Chak). In it the boundary between the two communities was set at the Bahr el-Arab/Kiir, this "being the boundary between the Anglo-Egyptian Sudan and Darfur". The Rizeigat were allowed to cross the river in order to hunt, but they were not permitted to bring their cattle to graze. By this agreement the government of Sudan also was protecting its territory from foreign encroachments.

The most surprising thing about this agreement was that despite the fact that it was recorded in the Sudan government's annual report – a hefty volume printed in London and sent to every provincial headquarters and government department – it was completely forgotten within six years of it being made. In 1918, following the Anglo-Egyptian conquest of Darfur, a new agreement was made between the Rizeigat and Malual which now defined the provincial boundary between Darfur and Bahr el-Ghazal, an internal administrative border within the Anglo-Egyptian Sudan. None of the British officials involved in this decision made any reference to the 1912 agreement and clearly knew nothing about it.

The key figure in this re-negotiation of the boundary was the British governor of Darfur, R.V. Savile, one of the most senior figures in the civil administration, who had been governor of Kordofan at the time of the conquest of Darfur, and then Darfur's first governor. The Rizeigat had allied with the British in the overthrow of sultan Ali Dinar, and there was a close relationship between Savile and Musa Madibbo. In fact they travelled to the border meeting together, and Savile purchased a horse from Madibbo on the way. At the border meeting, where Bahr el-Ghazal was represented not by their governor, but by a junior inspector who did not speak Dinka, Savile ruled in favour of the Rizeigat, declaring that the boundary between the two peoples was not the former international boundary at the Bahr el-Arab (as agreed in 1912), but forty miles to the south of the river. The intervening stretch he now declared was part of "Dar Rizeigat", and by extension annexed to Darfur, his province.

It should not surprise anyone that the Malual disputed this decision, and their dissatisfaction contributed to the rising of the Dinka in northern Bahr el-Ghazal in the early 1920s. The provincial government of Bahr el-Ghazal realized that the 1918 boundary had to be revised if they were to keep peace in their province. The politics of the border region had changed since 1918. The government still felt beholden to the Rizeigat because they had not joined the 1921 Nyala rising in southern Darfur, but this time the boundary meeting in 1924 was attended by the governors of both provinces: Major M.J. Wheatley of Bahr el-Ghazal and Patrick Munro of Darfur. The question confronting the two governors was not so much to decide who "owned" the land south of the river, but how to share the only available dry season grazing. Both communities needed access to the river in order for their cattle to survive. The agreement which bears the governors' names reduced the extent of "Dar Rizeigat" from forty to fourteen miles south of the river, recognized the right of the Malual to graze along a section of the south bank and fish in the river, but forbade the Rizeigat from entering Malual territory. It also established limits to Baggara grazing and hunting in the Western District (Kafia Kingi) of Bahr el-Ghazal.

This restriction on Rizeigat "Dar rights" appeared to settle the matter as far as the British administrators were concerned, but the Malual saw it only as a grazing agreement and refused to accept what they considered to be a land grab. Throughout the 1920s there were complaints about Rizeigat camps encroaching on Dinka grazing, and governor Wheatley even accused the Rizeigat of not adhering to the agreement. The Bahr el-Ghazal officials were beginning to learn more about the recent history of the Dinka, enough to dispute the claims presented by British officials in Darfur that Dar Rizeigat had always extended far south of the river. As one former army officer noted, "Before 1916 the Arabs did not graze South of the Bahr el Arab; except for raiding parties of Rizegat Arabs, no Arabs dared cross the River to graze, for the Dinkas would have gone for them."

The arguments raged back and forth between the Darfur and Bahr el-Ghazal administrations, and intensified after governors Wheatley and Munro retired and were replaced by men with no previous personal knowledge of the dispute. The Bahr el-Ghazal government had failed to keep adequate records of the pre-1924 situation, and of course Darfur's archive began only with the conquest of the province in 1916 (yet another example of the importance of maintaining an archive). They gave up trying to discover who had a prior claim to the river when some elderly Shatt men testified that their people had been there before either the Rizeigat or Malual, and the river really belonged to the Shatt.

The arguments continued throughout the 1930s. The district commissioner of northern Bahr el-Ghazal at one time proposed to confine the Rizeigat to the north bank of the river, and the district commissioner of Southern Darfur argued that the Dinka should be kept off the river entirely. The two provinces could not even agree on the name by which the agreement was called: Wheatley-Munro, or Munro-Wheatley. "Nobody wishes to re-open such a thorny subject as the Munro-Wheatley agreement," wrote the governor of Equatoria (which now included Bahr el-Ghazal) in 1938, but "it seems to me like the Versailles treaty, to hold the seeds of future war." The last twenty years "may have produced a set of circumstances which cannot be fully dealt with by reference to past history or the interpretation of agreements", and he urged a new arrangement to include expanding the grazing areas of both peoples by clearing tse-tse fly-infested land and sinking wells; thus relieving pressure on the border itself.

But governments never like to admit mistakes, and to reverse a decision is to admit a mistake. The civil secretary in Khartoum ruled in 1931 that the Wheatley-Munro agreement "must stand". Some tinkering with the arrangements for common grazing were made, but Darfur officials urged, "let us, by all means, seek a solution to the problem by exploring all possibilities in the way of improving grazing by digging wells and fighting fly, but do not let us precipitate matters by changing the existing state of affairs before economic or political reasons render alteration essential." The central government in Khartoum agreed that "the economic agreement needs a careful consideration and perhaps further inter-province negotiation", but it declined to intervene.

And that is where the matter rested throughout the rest of the condominium period. The Wheatley-Munro agreement has out lasted its authors and remains the basis of the boundary settlement along this section of what has now become an international border. It is a reminder that there is more to deciding boundaries than drawing lines on maps, and that border decisions must also include provisions for the livelihoods of border peoples if they are not to include the seeds of their own destruction.

Further reading:
>Gaim Kibreab, *State Intervention and the Environment in Sudan, 1889-1989*
>Douglas H. Johnson, *When Boundaries become Borders: the impact of boundary-making in southern Sudan's frontier zones*

33
HOW PART OF WESTERN BAHR EL-GHAZAL BECAME PART OF SOUTHERN DARFUR

Both the Addis Ababa Agreement and the Comprehensive Peace Agreement stipulate that the northern boundary of South Sudan should run along the provincial boundary lines as they were on Independence Day, 1 January 1956. There were not many formal changes to those lines after that date, but the biggest change, and so far the most contentious, was the annexation of the Hofret en-Nahas and Kafia Kingi areas of Bahr el-Ghazal's Western District to Darfur in 1960. In principle there should be no disagreement about the return of this district to Western Bahr el-Ghazal state. In practice there has been nothing but delay. How did this region become such a disputed hostage in the Addis Ababa Agreement and the CPA?

The Hofret en-Nahas–Kafia Kingi–Raga area of Western Bahr el-Ghazal is part of the region historically known as Dar Fartit. "Fartit" was a category applied by the Darfur Sultanate to numerous peoples from which slaves were taken; in effect "Fartit" means enslaveable people. Like the Nuba Mountains Dar Fartit was both targeted by and a refuge from expanding kingdoms and empires. It was included in Zubeir Pasha's trading empire in the mid-nineteenth century. It received many refugee groups fleeing the Dar Fur sultans to the north, the Azande advancing from the south, and French punitive campaigns across the western border in what is now the Central African Republic. As a result the population was of mixed origin, many small groups, some numbering only in the hundreds, speaking different languages, such as the Aja, Bai, Banda, Belanda-Bor, Belanda-Viri, Feroge, Kresh, Kara, Indiri, Njagulgule, Shatt, Thuri, and Yulu.

The area lies on the western edge of the ironstone plateau. It has numerous mahogany, teak and shea forests, and is crossed by many seasonal rivers and khors running north–north-east from the Nile-Congo Watershed to the river systems feeding into the Bahr el-Arab/Kiir river. The river valleys became the homes to specific refugee groups, so that the linguistic map of the region came to resemble its hydrological map as well.

Slaves were not the only resource that attracted persons from Darfur to the area. Hofrat en-Nahas means 'copper pit' in Arabic, and it was once mined for copper and other minerals by prospectors operating out of Darfur. During the nineteenth and twentieth centuries bands of hunters would also enter the area in search of ivory and animal skins. The region's forests of tropical hardwoods would become an important export resource later in the twentieth and twenty-first centuries.

After the Anglo-Egyptian authorities reclaimed Bahr el-Ghazal in 1901 Western Bahr el-Ghazal District became one of the most remote areas administered by Sudan. A road eventually linked Wau, the province capital, to Raga, Kafia Kingi and Hofrat en-Nahas. British administrators' main concern in the early years of the twentieth century was to prevent slave-trading from across the border with the independent Darfur Sultanate, and to try to control the influx of refugees from the French territories to the west. Disturbances within the Darfur Sultanate up to 1916, when it was conquered and re-incorporated into Sudan, also produced a flow of refugees fleeing Sultan 'Ali Dinar's rule. These peoples were mainly Muslim, as were many of the other inhabitants of the district, and were bilingual in Arabic and their indigenous language, as were many of the peoples in the region.

This was the situation in this remote and neglected district for the first thirty years of Anglo-Egyptian rule. The announcement of the "Southern Policy" in 1930 brought a dramatic change. The Southern Policy outlined the application of Native Administration in the southern provinces as the incorporation of native institutions and customs into local administration, and in particular developing the people of the South along "African", as opposed to "Middle Eastern" lines (chapter 1). The governor of Bahr el-Ghazal, Major Roy Gerard Corcor Brock, approached administration along military lines and applied a strict interpretation of this policy to the Western District. In order to segregate the "African" from the "Arab" inhabitants of the district he ordered the expulsion of the Darfur immigrants back to Darfur and forcibly resettled the rest of the population along the road to Raga. A "No-Man's Land" was created along the border with Darfur, Hofrat en-Nahas and Kafia Kingi stations were closed, and abandoned villages were burned down. The peoples resettled near Raga were instructed to stop wearing Muslim dress and to abandon any Arabic names they had adopted. The speaking of Arabic, however, continued, as it was the only language common to all groups, and the only language with which they could communicate with provincial administrators.

Sudanese nationalists have cited the destruction of Hofrat en-Nahas and Kafia Kingi as typical of the Southern Policy. In fact the civil secretary, Harold MacMichael was taken by surprise at this extreme application of the general principles he had announced. The governor of Darfur was outraged to be loaded with a large number of destitute refugees expelled from Bahr el-Ghazal and protested vigorously. But provincial governors in those days had considerable autonomy and Brock's decision was allowed to stand.

The depopulation of Hofrat en-Nahas and Kafia Kingi had environmental consequences. The former inhabitants had been cultivators and had cleared substantial areas for agriculture. As these cultivations returned to the bush, so the tse-tse fly belt also advanced into areas that had long been fly-free. With the tse-tse fly came the cattle disease trypanosomiasis. Peaceful administration along the border meant that pastoralists from Darfur, mainly the Rizeigat, now regularly took their cattle south into Bahr el-Ghazal for seasonal grazing, but were confronted by the spread of "tryps". One solution discussed by administrators was to allow the return of the former inhabitants to reclaim the bush for agriculture; thus acting as "fly swatters for the Rizeigat". But it was not until the late 1940s when the Southern Policy was rescinded and Sudanese independence was in the offing that Kafia Kingi and Hofrat en-Nahas were repopulated.

By this time both Bahr el-Ghazal and Darfur provinces had an interest in how the Western District was administered. In 1946, shortly before the Southern Policy was rescinded, Darfur was offered the district but declined to take it on because it was too remote. The governor described his province's policy towards the district as preserving Darfur's hunting and grazing rights while refusing to assume administrative responsibility. In other words he asserted the rights of the southern Darfur peoples to the seasonal use of a district that remained beyond Darfur's jurisdiction.

Hofrat en-Nahas and Kafia Kingi were part of the Western District, Bahr el-Ghazal on Independence Day, 1 January 1956. Independence brought no immediate change to provincial or national policy towards the district, but after the 1958 Abboud coup Khartoum began investigating the mineral potential of the region, and in 1960 redrew the provincial boundaries to include in Darfur Hofrat en-Nahas and Kafia Kingi up to the River Rikki. By this time a number of Binga, Masalit and Habbaniya peoples had moved into the area from Darfur, as well as West African immigrants such as the Bornu, Fellata and Bagirma. There was, however, local resentment at the boundary change, but because Sudan was now under a military regime there was little chance of expressing this resentment. The transfer of Kafia Kingi to Darfur motivated some persons later to join the Anyanya when it reached Raga county in 1964.

The Addis Ababa Agreement of 1972 stipulated that the borders of the newly formed Southern Region would follow the provincial boundaries as they were on 1 January 1956, and a committee formed in Raga and Wau formally requested the return of the Kafia Kingi enclave in 1974, and the High Executive Committee in Juba appointed a committee to oversee the handover in 1981. But groups in Darfur equally wanted to retain Kafia Kingi. President Nimeiri issued a presidential decree restoring Kafia Kingi to Bahr el-Ghazal, but secretly instructed the governor of Darfur region, Ahmed Diraige, to delay its implementation. Kafia Kingi remained part of Darfur by the time the second civil war broke out in 1983.

The current government in Khartoum has signed two agreements that use the 1956 boundary to define the northern border of South Sudan: the Khartoum Peace Agreement in 1997, and the Comprehensive Peace Agreement in 2005. The government's submission on Abyei to the Permanent Court of Arbitration in The Hague also recognized the 1956 boundary line for the Kafia Kingi enclave. There are strong voices in Darfur opposing the transfer of either Hofrat en-Nahas or the rest of the Kafia Kingi enclave to South Sudan. The issue remained unresolved by the time South Sudan achieved its formal independence on 9 July 2011.

Further reading
    Edward Thomas, *The Kafia Kingi Enclave: people, politics and history in the north-south boundary zone of western Sudan*

34
HOW CHALI AND YABUS LEFT THE SOUTH

The people of Chali el-Fil and Yabus, who are now part of Blue Nile state, were at one time included in Upper Nile. Collectively known as Burun by the Arabs and Cai by the Nuer, the Uduk and Koma peoples have much in common with their Mabaan neighbours, who inhabit the north-eastern corner of Upper Nile. Throughout the last two centuries they have lived on multiple frontiers between Sudan and Ethiopia, and Sudan and South Sudan.

In the nineteenth century this region bordering the Ethiopian foothills passed back and forth between the Turco-Egyptian empire, Ethiopia and the Anglo-Egyptian Sudan. As well as frontier garrisons there were also local hill sheikhs controlling their own mini-states. A number of them based their economy in part on slave-raiding and the Koma, Uduk, Mabaan, and other "Burun" were the main victims. By the end of the nineteenth century, when the Anglo-Egyptian forces entered the region, these people lived in scattered villages, often on hill tops, where it was reported that because of persistent slave-raiding, in which women and children were the main targets, the men outnumbered the women.

The new Anglo-Egyptian government wanted to bring these border disturbances to an end, and in defining the international border between Sudan and Ethiopia made sure that the headquarters of some of the biggest slave-raiders were included in Sudan. In 1904 a military expedition to Jebel Jerok captured Muhammad wad Mahmud, one of the most notorious slavers, who was taken back to Medani and hanged. Border outposts were then set up to prevent further raiding, the most important being established at Jebel Kurmuk in 1910. People began to return to the area, restoring old villages or founding new ones from north of Khor Tombak to south of the Yabus. One of the most important trading villages was Jalei, which British officers pronounced and wrote as "Chali".

It was one thing to secure the border, but it was another thing to administer the frontier area now contained within that border. A road was built to connect Kurmuk with Roseires, and for some time Kurmuk was the main administrative headquarters. But this region flanked Upper Nile Province as well as Ethiopia. Given the scattered nature of the peoples and their villages administrators fretted that any provincial boundary line would be arbitrary.

And so it turned out to be. Wherever the line was drawn administrators had to deal with a problem of access, as the frontier remained remote from the main lines of river and road communication. In 1917 when the governor of Upper Nile wanted to investigate reports that the Nuer of his province had been raiding the Mabaan (reports that later proved false), he had to travel through the neighbouring province to reach the Mabaan, rather than overland from Nasir on the Sobat. A slight boundary adjustment was made in the mid-1920s to include the Koma of the Daga valley in the Eastern District administered from Nasir, but the main change came in 1938 when all of the Koma, the Uduk and the Mabaan were finally incorporated into Upper Nile Province.

This was to have a profound impact on at least the Uduk and Mabaan. When the American missionaries of the Sudan Interior Mission (SIM) were expelled from Ethiopia by the Italians after 1936, they moved their operation to Sudan. British officials did not allow missions to be set up in northern "Muslim" provinces; nor did they want American missionaries active among the larger and more politically important southern Sudanese communities. For both these reasons the SIM were shunted off to a remote frontier where it was thought they could do the least harm. This is how mission stations came to be set up at Chali among the Uduk and Doro among the Mabaan, and how both the Uduk and Mabaan languages came to be written, and small Christian communities came to be founded.

The boundary change was not to be permanent, though the influence of the missions was. During World War Two both mission stations found themselves on the frontline between Britain and Italy, and the mission station at Doro was even bombed by the Italians, killing three American missionaries. A motor road was constructed south from Kurmuk, paralleling the international border. Things returned to normal after the defeat of the Italians, and for a while the three border peoples of Mabaan, Uduk and Koma were administered from Renk on the White Nile, the northern-most district headquarters in Upper Nile.

Though a road from Paloich did connect Chali to the main north-south road running between Renk and Malakal, it was still closer to Kurmuk than Renk, and the wartime motor road made it more accessible to Kurmuk as well. In 1953, just over two years before the independence of Sudan, an internal reorganization of Blue Nile province meant the creation of two new districts: Northern and Southern Fung, with the Uduk of Chali and the Koma of Yabus Bridge being incorporated into Southern Fung district and reattached to the Kurmuk sub-district. The date of this transfer was to acquire great significance for the peoples living on either side of the new border.

The people of Chali were affected indirectly by the civil war being fought just south of them in Upper Nile during the 1960s. The SIM missionaries were among those expelled by the Khartoum government in 1964, but the Chali and Doro churches continued to be run by local pastors and their congregations. No fighting spilled over into Blue Nile, but the Addis Ababa Agreement of 1972 raised a new possibility. The agreement, and the organic law based on it, defined the Southern Region as the three southern provinces "in accordance with their boundaries as they stood on January 1, 1956, and any other areas that were culturally and geographically a part of the Southern complex as may be decided by a referendum." It was the last clause that assumed immediate significance, because it appeared to offer a way by which the people of Chali and Yabus might rejoin their neighbours in Upper Nile.

Unfortunately, whatever the letter of the law stated, the implementation was different. A number of Uduk petitioned the government to hold a referendum to decide whether they would rejoin the Southern Region, but they were arrested. One, Shadrack Peyko Dhunya, had to leave Blue Nile and move to Wau, where he became the headmaster of a school until his death shortly before the end of the second civil war. The Uduk church leaders were the focus of government suspicion even before the outbreak of civil war in 1983.

With the outbreak of war Chali and the Uduk once again found themselves on the frontline. In 1986 the SPLA began recruiting in their area, and in 1987 the Sudanese army began burning their villages in retaliation. Most of the Uduk became refugees and moved en masse into Ethiopia. The SPLA secured the southern Funj area after taking Kurmuk in 1997, but most of the Uduk remained refugees in Ethiopia until after the end of the war. The provisions of the Comprehensive Peace Ageement were not as generous to the people of southern Blue Nile as the Addis Ababa Agreement had been in principle. Now the 1956 provincial boundaries became a rigid dividing line between them and South Sudan, with no option for those "culturally and geographically a part of the Southern complex" to have their own referendum.

The fighting in Blue Nile state that began in 2011 is a direct result of a series of arbitrary border decisions. The Mabaan and Uduk were transferred to Upper Nile together in 1938, but only the Maban remain "South Sudanese" because they were retained in Upper Nile when the border was redrawn 1953. The Koma people remain divided between Upper Nile and Blue Nile, between South Sudan and Sudan. The new international border is no less arbitrary than the old provincial boundaries.

Further reading:
> Wendy James, *War and Survival in Sudan's Frontier Lands: voices from the Blue Nile*

LEGACIES

35
WHY DO WE NEED ARCHIVES?

"Why do we need a room to keep old records?" This was the comment of a very senior member of the High Executive Council reported to me more than thirty years ago. At that time I was assistant director for archives in the Regional Ministry of Information and Culture, and the director, Lawrence Modi Tombe, and I had spent the best part of two years trying to persuade the Southern Regional Government to allocate a building to house a Southern Regional Records Office and provide the regional government with a proper archive service. In this we failed. The attitude of the official quoted above was widespread. Despite the fact that each regional ministry was generating piles of correspondence, forms, reports and folders (not to mention the documents being produced by each provincial government), little thought was given to creating an efficient way to store and retrieve the information contained in these records. We never got a building, and the Southern Regional Government never got its archive.

The idea for an archive for the Southern Regional Government originated with late Mading de Garang, then Regional Minister for Information and Culture, Wildlife and Tourism. He established a department of archives in 1977, taking over the responsibility of the closed files kept in the basement of the former Equatoria Province Mudiriyya (now the headquarters for Central Equatoria State). The intention was to collect further closed files from all of the South's district and provincial headquarters, but no systematic collection of files from undertaken until 1981-3.

My familiarity with these "old records" began during my doctoral research in Upper Nile and Jonglei provinces in the 1970s. The provincial commissioners of Upper Nile, late Peter Gatkuoth Gual and Philip Obang were very hospitable to my research, which was on the history of the peoples of Upper Nile, and did everything in their power to facilitate it. I had full access to the provincial records stored in Malakal where I found documents dating as far as back 1904, reports on the origins of administrative policies, discussions about the application of customary law, grazing agreements, delineations of district and province boundaries, personality reports on chiefs and other prominent southern Sudanese, even instructions on practical matters such as the design of mosquito proof houses and how to make bricks from Upper Nile's clay soil.

My main task when I came to Juba as Assistant Director of Archives was to transfer provincial records to Juba, which could only be done during the dry season. I managed to transfer over 5000 government files from Malakal, Torit, Yambio, Ezo, Tembura, Bor, Pibor, Akobo, New Fangak, and Nasir. These ranged in date from the early twentieth century up to the signing of the Addis Ababa Agreement in 1972. We still had no single building for all these records, and many had to be stored in beer cartons (Tusker Export was just the right size for the government folders).

On redivision in 1983 the Southern Regional Records Office remained in Juba, under the authority of the Equatoria Regional Government. It has to be said that this authority failed to perform its responsibility to preserve this heritage for the rest of South Sudan. The archive collection was split up between several different buildings, moved about as these buildings were allocated for different purposes, often dumped in disorder in poorly maintained storerooms, left to be eaten by termites, nibbled by rodents, fouled by bats, and soaked in puddles of rain water. The attitude of some regional officials was that this archive was "a big headache", as one of them put it to me when I returned to Juba in 2006.

Whatever the state of the archives in Juba throughout the civil war, the fate of government records left in the district headquarters was far worse. Between 1990 and 1996 I worked on and off in Operation Lifeline Sudan and was able to visit many of the places I had known during the Addis Ababa peace. I found that soldiers – whether from the government or the SPLA – seemed to make war on paper wherever they went. Nothing survived of the current records I had left behind in various headquarters. Even in towns held by the government throughout the war records were often put to other uses by soldiers, most commonly as cigarette paper. Very little survives of an administrative record that used to cover nearly a century of southern Sudan's history.

The negotiations for the Comprehensive Peace Agreement brought an opportunity to halt the neglect and destruction of the South's heritage. In 2004 representatives of the British Institute in Eastern Africa and I met with late Samson Kwaje at Naivasha and discussed with him plans for reviving the archive and setting up a proper antiquities and museum service. These plans began to be implemented by John Luk when he was Minister for Culture, and today are finally bearing fruit.

It takes money, training and commitment to build an archive service. Unlike thirty years ago the money and commitment is there, and this is making the training possible. Different agencies – USAID and the US Ambassadors Cultural Fund – provided funds for the initial revival of the archives, and research institutions – the British Institute in Eastern Africa and the Rift Valley Institute – have been providing the training.

Why is this all necessary? A well-regulated archive is the responsibility of every modern government. It serves as a repository for official documents recording the context and reasons for past administrative decisions, the data on which different government departments base their work, information on which development projects can be constructed, and historical and cultural information of value to the general public and academic researchers alike.

The elements necessary for a well regulated archive are: legislation setting out clearly the authority for the protection, preservation, and public access of public records; internal regulations for the regular transfer and release of documents to the archive; buildings for the secure and safe storage of documents; a trained professional staff charged with the responsibility for preserving documents and making them accessible; and a suitable financial structure for maintaining the archive.

These are the general principles, but what does this archive have to offer South Sudan? After all, many of these old records were produced not by South Sudanese, but by foreigners. In the first place they contain practical information that can still be of use. These records document the founding of the administrative system still operating in the rural areas and detail the reasons for creating that system, what worked, what didn't, and why. They often record information that could have been used, and could still be used, in the implementation of the CPA, because many of the records I brought back from Malakal in 1981 and 1983 documented the provincial boundaries of the old Upper Nile Province, which of course is relevant to the definition and demarcation of the north-south border. Unfortunately the negligent way in which these files were stored after 1983 means that many of these records have been lost or destroyed, and a search is still underway to locate what has survived.

In addition to this practical information there is the historical information of value to South Sudanese as they begin to research and interpret their own past. Some of the files that have survived record the activities of persons who later became prominent in the South's recent history: Akuot Atem as a police sergeant stopping a tribal fight in the early 1950s; the record of Joseph Oduho's employment as a teacher; Buth Diu's trial in the late 1950s for publicly advocating federalism, a political solution, which if adopted then might have avoided the two civil wars the South suffered since.

But if this archive is kept in Juba, can it be used by persons in the other states? Fortunately, new technology means that it can. In the early 1980s there was no photocopying facility in Juba. Whenever I found a document that was interesting I would make a copy by typing it out on my portable typewriter. Today digital technology means that original documents can be scanned, saved on hard drives, copied onto CDs or memory sticks, and sent back to the states from which they originated. In the future digitized documents could even be posted online. The Rift Valley Institute has provided the archive with equipment and training to establish a digital laboratory and have begun digitizing documents dealing with the South's regional, internal and international borders.

What still needs to be done? South Sudan could have a fully functioning archive service: it has the equipment, it has staff who are being trained and are enthusiastic and dedicated to the job, it has the support of external agencies and some foreign donors. What it needs is a building in which to store the documents safely, undertake repairs of damaged records, continue digitization, and provide a place where the documents can be consulted. And this needs the commitment of the Government of South Sudan to allocate the resources and provide the necessary budget – something the old regional governments failed to do.

As the South faces a new future, let it also pay attention to and preserve its past.

36
HOW RECORDS WERE KEPT IN SOUTH SUDAN

In August 1921 the deputy governor of Upper Nile in Malakal wrote an urgent letter to the civil secretary in Khartoum. The civil secretary was in charge of the civil administration throughout Sudan, second only to the governor-general. He was usually concerned with matters of policy, of how the country was run, but the matter the deputy governor needed help on was something more mundane: the filing system. "Clerks come here without any sort of training in methods of card indexing, filing or registration", he complained. "Everything is lumped under General." He then detailed the scale of the difficulty, "I sent for the U.N.P. General file as a matter of curiosity: it took two murasalas just over ten minutes to bring it in, making a journey every thirty seconds."

The contents of the "General" files were indeed very general, and he found no subject classification or order. To illustrate the chaos he listed the contents of a single file, one titled "Route Reports 204". "There were no route reports", he reported, but rather some sixty-six different unrelated subjects, including: issue of rations to felucca boys, Tonga resthouse, boys for Khartoum workshops, Renk police, pay for Nuer syce, marking rifles, uncensored letters, disposal of slave cases, Xmas salutations from the Sirdar, permits to trade up the Zeraf, corrugated iron for wells, Nuers in hospital, allotment of pay to soldier's wives, wooden cart from meshra, rainfall at Malakal, indent for 20 axes, approval to sell old merkaz mule (with large sore on penis), enforcement of plimsoll line, theft of waterproof sheets, sick Nuers for hospital, province officials getting into debt, Sudan Government Railway timetables for 1918, Ful Sudan rates for 1916, receipt for military buff adjustable chinstraps, Nuer interpreter for slave dealing, dress for Egyptian Officers and Officials, postage of unpaid correspondence, El Obeid station resthouse, attack by Nuers on Buruns, and various odd pieces of paper in English and Arabic.

The civil cecretary, Harold MacMichael, was sympathetic and sent some brief guidelines, adding "*Never* have a 'General' or 'Various' or 'Miscellaneous' file: it ruins everything." But the problem of the filing system wasn't confined to Malakal. Shortly after replying to Upper Nile's deputy governor MacMichael issued a memo to his own staff in Khartoum. "The present state of affairs in the office as regards registering and indexing is unsatisfactory", he complained. "If files are to be traceable it is absolutely essential their SUBJECT should be properly marked on them. If the subject is unsuitably worded it is impossible to find the file."

The problem was a legacy of the military that dominated administration throughout the first half of the Condominium. The military needed to produce and keep records, just like any other institution, but each office and department seemed to keep records in different ways. In the years immediately preceding the Re-conquest the military intelligence department consolidated reports from the field and circulated them in printed form, initially in the *Intelligence Report, Egypt* series, which became the *Sudan Intelligence Report* after the Battle of Omdurman. These compiled reports continued to be produced and circulated to provincial and departmental offices throughout the first three decades of the twentieth century, but their contents, too, could be quite general. The report for April 1908, for instance, contained a list of sheikhs visiting Khartoum from Suakin, a report of the route from Bor to the Murle country, monthly reports from Meridi, a history of Kordofan before the Egyptian conquest, a report on the country between Bara and Omdurman, a report on Jebel Nyima in the Nuba mountains, and a report on the Egyptian province of the Sinai. Before World War One reports circulated this way through the *Sudan Intelligence Report* continued to be full, if miscellaneous. But during the war this form of reporting declined and by 1921, the year of the Upper Nile Province deputy governor's cry for help, the monthly reports had virtually ceased to reproduce full reports at all and were confined to publishing news summaries.

At least these reports were formal. Correspondence to and from the governor-general was often less so. Until 1925 the governor-general of Sudan was also the commander-in-chief (or Sirdar) of the entire Egyptian army (not just the army in Sudan), and his correspondence on civil and military matters often overlapped. Wingate, the longest serving governor-general (1899-1916), often conducted his correspondence with his provincial governors (all of them British officers in the Egyptian army) in hand-written, informal letters. These were not neatly filed away in folders with labelled subject headings, but kept as his personal correspondence (and can now be read, along with more formal typed letters and reports, in the Sudan Archive in the University of Durham). When Wingate left Khartoum in 1916 to become Agent and Consul General in Egypt, he took this correspondence with him, leaving a gaping hole in the official record. This was not uncommon during the first two decades of the century. The departure of senior officials such as provincial governors, as they were rotated out of the Egyptian army and back to their home regiments, often left huge gaps in the institutional memory of administration, and it was not uncommon for new governors to claim to have no knowledge of the policies of their more distant predecessors.

The 1920s saw Sudan's civil administration emerging from military domination, bringing with it more bureaucratic ways of operating. Most provincial governors were now civilians, and the civil secretary was now the main point of contact between the provincial and central governments, unlike the days of Wingate when all senior officers reported directly to the sirdar/governor-general. Harold MacMichael, the most influential of all Sudan's civil secretaries, was also one of its most scholarly administrators. His field reports often cited ancient geographers and historians and were reprinted in scholarly journals in Britain. The civil secretary's filing system produced in the 1920s in response to such cries for help as that coming from Malakal was methodical as well as flexible. Each main subject was given a number, each sub-division a letter, and each further sub-division another number. Thus Personnel files (number 50 in the filing system) had a number of sub-divisions ranging from General Rulings (A) and Senior Staff (B) on down to Southern Staff (Z), and each individual staff member would be given a separate number. So, a hypothetical southern sub-mamur named Zakaria Fulan might have a personnel file in Khartoum numbered 50 (Personnel) Z (Southern Staff) 36 (Zakaria Fulan), with another file of the exact same number in his office of employment. This filing system, where the file numbers were included on each piece of correspondence, meant that duplicate files could be compiled of correspondence between the provinces and Khartoum, or province capitals and their districts, and even between province capitals, so that records could be easily retrieved and added to.

The numbering system followed a broadly alphabetical sequence: Administration (1), Agriculture (2), Antiquities (3), Arms & Ammunition (4), Army (5), Audit (6), Aviation (7), Boundaries (8), Buildings (9) and so on. At least 112 separate subject numbers were allocated, though a strict alphabetical system was abandoned once the letter V was reached in the 60s (Veterinary – 68, Visits & Inspections – 69). Town Improvements (90) was followed by Film Making in Sudan (92), Abyssinian Frontier Affairs (93), Nile Research (99) and Anthropological & Historical Research (112).

Of course the initial allocation of subject titles in the 1920s could not anticipate the way these subjects might develop. Clubs & Societies, file number 10, was originally intended for the registration of social clubs such as the Sudan Club, Catholic Club and Armenian Club in Khartoum, or the Greek Club in Juba, as well as sporting clubs, such as the Blue Nile Yacht Club. But it was also became the file number for reports on political parties and the so-called "secret societies" of the Azande and other subversive organizations.

There was also considerable overlap and cross-filing between subjects. Tribal (66) contained routine correspondence as well as substantive reports on issues of tribal administration, and each tribe had its own series of files. Some of these reports might also be copied under (1) Administration, (36) Intelligence (where reports on political parties and seditious movements might also be found), (56) Reports, and finally, (112) Anthropological & Historical research. It is in the latter category that copies of some of the oldest reports can sometimes be found – reports that otherwise would have been lost in the primordial chaos of the first years of civil administration.

The civil secretary's filing system is not just a matter of historical or academic interest. It continued to be used, with some modifications, right through the formation and dissolution of the Southern Region, and is the basis of the filing system of the ministries today. All the more reason why South Sudan should take care to preserve, maintain, and add to its national archive.

37
IS THERE A ROLE FOR THE AMATEUR HISTORIAN IN SOUTH SUDAN?

"Is there a role for the amateur historian in South Sudan?" my friend Jacob Akol asked me. The conversation that led to this question had begun with another. "I'd really like to know who killed Ayok Lual," he said. This was a question I could not answer, since I did not know who Ayok Lual was. So he told me the story he had heard since his school days.

Ayok Lual was chief of the Aguok section of the Rek Dinka and lived at Marial Aguok, north of what is now Gogrial town. In the nineteenth century two of the most notorious slavers in the area were a Dinka called Lual Ngor (possibly from Apuk area) and a Jallaba (Arab) called Abdallah, who was given the additional Dinka "bull name" of Manyiel. Abdallah Manyiel had his zariba (fortified camp) at Wutuur just west of Gogrial town, and his headquarters zariba at Bundiir further west of Wuntuur, from where he carried out raids up to and across the Bahr el-Ghazal.

Lual Ngor was in league with slave-traders who gave him guns, and with these guns he raised his own army. He was so arrogant and so sure of his powers that he immortalized his name in the saying: "Even a man who will never die says Lual Ngor cannot do that!" The people of Apuk and Aguok came together, defeated his army and killed him. They then scattered his children, sending them to live with other families, so that Lual Ngor's lineage would die out.

Abdallah Manyiel met a similar fate when the combined forces of Aguok and Apuk, led by main clans of the Spear Masters (*bany biith*), including the Payi Clan of Ayok Lual, stormed his zeribas at Wuntuur and Bundiir. It is not clear if he was killed at the Battle of Wunttuur or Battle of Bundiir. What adds to his notoriety is the myth that when the victors opened his stomach to make sure he was dead they found a live catfish swimming in his stomach.

Some time after this a steamer landed a force of armed men at Majok Amaal, a small river port or landing place about seven miles north of Gogrial town on the river Jur. The force was described as being composed of black men who were neither Dinka nor Arab. This force captured a local man at Majok Amaal and forced him to lead them to the village and home of Ayok. They left in the evening and arrived at Ayok Lual's village of Marial Aguok before sunrise, at about five in the morning. They told Ayok that they were taking him to Wau to add the chieftaincy of Book Alok to his own. When they left word went out that the armed force had taken the chief, so people began to gather and shadow them.

At sunrise the force reached Alek, about ten miles north of Gogrial. There Ayok Lual suddenly sat down and refused to go any further, telling his captors that if they wanted to kill him, they could do so here. He was shot dead, whereupon the force was attacked from all sides by Dinka warriors who had hidden in the surrounding millet cultivations. The force were armed with guns that fired exploding bullets, something like grenades, which left marks where they hit the trunks of the palm trees. Despite the use of this weapon the force was nearly annihilated, with only a few escaping back to the river. Jacob remembered being taken to Alek as part of a school party and being shown the marks from the battle still visible on the trees in the mid 1950s.

The death of Ayok Lual and its aftermath, as far as I know, has never before been written down. There might be contemporary nineteenth-century sources that can help us date the event or identify the force that captured Ayok Lual: possibly the army of one of the larger merchant-princes, such as Zubair Pasha. They were known to be armed with large bore elephant guns that had to be fired from a tripod and shot grenade-like exploding bullets.

If we are able to link up this account with contemporary sources it would add new detail to our knowledge of the activities of slave-raiders – both foreign and local – in the Bahr el-Ghazal, and their impact on specific communities.

This example demonstrates the important contribution amateur historians in South Sudan can make. Most of what we know about South Sudan's past came originally from the oral testimony of its own people. What British administrators wrote down in their reports, and which is preserved in the archives, was based on what local people told them. Professional historians also base their work on local testimony. They may make use of written sources inaccessible to most South Sudanese, and they may have developed techniques for establishing the dating and chronology of events that amateur historians might lack, but in the end they are doing the same thing: collecting the oral testimony of indigenous communities in order to reconstruct the events of the past.

The collection of such historical accounts should not be a haphazard. It is important when collecting such testimony to make a note of the circumstances in which it is told, who the teller is, his (or her) age or age-set (if they have one), what community they come from, what is their authority for the account they are giving. If the testimony is being recorded first in the vernacular language before being translated, it is always important to retain the vernacular words for kinship, social, and religious terms. The Arabic word "kujur" for instance, is applied to a wide variety of spiritual and not-so-spiritual figures and should never be used to translate vernacular terms. Much also can be learned about the past from the recording of songs, which often have allusions to historic events.

Any interpretive history needs to date events and place them in a chronology, something that is difficult to do for societies that have no calendar. I have seen some texts by local historians that attribute events to "the medieval period", or the fifteenth, sixteenth, or seventeenth centuries, with no explanation of how these dates are calculated. It is important not to be over-enthusiastic in attributing dates, but there are ways of constructing a chronology partly from oral testimony. Many societies will name years after special events, such as floods, epidemics or battles. Some have age-sets with regulated times for opening and closing. Those lucky few societies (purely from the historian's point of view) with kingship have lines of succession that can give estimated dates.

To answer the question posed above, the amateur historian does have an important role to play in South Sudan. Professional historians working on South Sudan, so far, are few, and they are able to research only a few communities at a time. There are active local history societies in countries like Britain and the United States that delve into the past of communities often overlooked by professional historians. In some senses all history is local, and the work of amateur historians should be an important contribution to recovering the South Sudan's past. As South Sudan trains more of its own professional historians, let them remember the work of amateur historians as well.

SELECTED READING

P.G.M.B., "Il Rev. P. Daniele Sorur. Nero della tribù dei Denka. Missionario dell'Africa Centrale", *Nigrizia* (1900)

Robert O. Collins, *Shadows in the Grass: Britain in the southern Sudan 1918-1956* (New Haven: Yale University Press, 1983)

Robert O. Collins, *The Waters of the Nile: hydropolitics and the Jonglei Canal 1900-1988* (Oxford: Oxford University Press, 1990)

Fr. Dellagiacoma (ed.), *How a Slave became a Minister: autobiography of sayyed Stanislaus Abdallahi Paysama* (Khartoum, 1990)

Fr. Daniel Surur Farim Deng, "Memorie scritte dal R. P. Daniele Sorur Pharim Dèn", *Nigrizia* (1887-1888)

Fr. Daniel Surur Farim Deng, "A Dinka priest writing on his own People", in Elias Toniolo and Richard Hill (eds), *The Opening of the Nile Basin* (London, 1974)

Christopher Ehret, *The Civilizations of Africa: a history to 1800* (Charlottesville, VA: University of Virginia Press, 2002)

E. E. Evans-Pritchard, *Nuer Religion* (Oxford: Clarendon Press, 1956)

E. E. Evans-Pritchard, *Theories of Primitive Religion* (Oxford: Clarendon Press, 1965)

Richard Gray, *A History of the Southern Sudan 1839-1889* (London: Oxford University Press, 1961)

Joseph Greenberg, *The Languages of Africa* (Bloomington: Indiana University Press, 1966)

Richard L. Hill, *Egypt in the Sudan 1820-1881* (London: Oxford University Press, 1959)

Richard Hill and Peter Hogg, *A Black Corps d'Élite: an Egyptian Sudanese conscript battalion with the French army in Mexico, 1863-1867, and its survivors in subsequent African history* (East Lansing MI: Michigan State University Press, 1995)

P.M.Holt, *The Mahdist State in the Sudan 1881-1898: a study of its origins, development and overthrow*, 2nd ed. (Oxford: Clarendon Press, 1970)

Paul Howell, Mike Lock & Stephen Cobb (eds), *The Jonglei Canal: impact and opportunity* (Cambridge: Cambridge University Press, 1988)

Wendy James, *War and Survival in Sudan's Frontier Lands: voices from the Blue Nile* (Oxford: Oxford University Press, 2007)

Douglas H. Johnson, "Divinity abroad: Dinka missionaries in foreign lands", in Wendy James & Douglas H. Johnson (eds), *Vernacular Christianity: essays on the social anthropology of religion presented to Godfrey Lienhardt* JASO Occasional Papers No. 7 (Oxford/New York: JASO/Lilian Barber Press, 1988)

Douglas H. Johnson, "The 1954 Juba conference, also known as the Both Diu conference", *Southern Sudan Post* (January 2007)

Douglas H. Johnson, "The prophet Ngundeng and the battle of Pading: prophecy, symbolism and historical evidence", in David M. Anderson and Douglas H. Johnson (eds), *Revealing Prophets: prophecy in Eastern African history* (London: James Currey, 1995)

Douglas H. Johnson, *Nuer Prophets: history and prophecy from the Upper Nile* (Oxford: Clarendon Press, 1994)

Douglas H. Johnson, "Salim Wilson: the black evangelist of the north", *Journal of Religion in Africa*, 21/1 (1991)

Douglas H. Johnson, "Salim Charles Wilson", *Dictionary of National Biography* (Oxford: Oxford University Press, 2011)

Douglas H. Johnson (ed.), *Sudan, 1942-1950,* British Documents on the End of Empire, Series B, Volume 5, part I (London: The Stationery Office, 1998)

Douglas H. Johnson (ed.), *Sudan, 1951-1956*, British Documents on the End of Empire Series B, volume 5, part II (London: The Stationery Office, 1998)

Douglas H. Johnson, "Tribal boundaries and border wars: Nuer–Dinka relations in the Sobat and Zaraf valleys, c. 1860-1976", *Journal of African History* 23/2 (1982)

Douglas H. Johnson, "Tribe or nationality? The Sudanese diaspora and the Kenyan Nubis", *Journal of Eastern African Studies*, 3/1 (2009)

Douglas H. Johnson, *When Boundaries become Borders: the impact of boundary-making in southern Sudan's frontier zones* (London & Nairobi: Rift Valley Institute, 2010)

Douglas H. Johnson, "Zenab, Caterina", *Dictionary of African Biography*, volume 6 (New York: Oxford University Press, 2011)

Gaim Kibreab, *State Intervention and the Environment in Sudan, 1889-1989* (Lewiston, NY & Lampeter, UK: Edwin Mellen Press, 2002)

Yoshiko Kurita, *'Ali 'Abd al-Latif wa Thawra 1924* [in Arabic: Ali Abd al-Latif and the Revolution of 1924] (Cairo: Sudanese Studies Centre, 1997)

Ronald L. Lamothe, *Slaves of Fortune: Sudanese soldiers and the River War, 1896-98* (Woodbridge: James Currey, 2011)

Paul Lane and Douglas H. Johnson, "The archaeology and history of slavery in South Sudan in the nineteenth century", in Andrew Peacock (ed.) *The Frontiers of the Ottoman World, Proceedings of the British Academy*, 156 (2009)

R. G. Lienhardt, *Divinity and Experience: the religion of the Dinka* (Oxford: Clarendon Press, 1961)

P. Machell, "Memoirs of a Sudanese soldier (Ali Effendi Gifoon)", *Cornhill Magazine*, Series 3, volume I, numbers 439-442 (July-October 1896)

Lilian Passmore Sanderson & Neville Sanderson, *Education, Religion & Politics in Southern Sudan 1899-1964* (London: Ithaca Press, 1981)

Edward Thomas, *The Kafia Kingi Enclave: people, politics and history in the north-south boundary zone of western Sudan* (London & Nairobi: Rift Valley Institute, 2010)

Elena Vezzadini, *Lost Nationalism: memory, insurgency, and revolutionary departures in colonial Sudan* (Woodbridge: James Currey, 2015)

Dunstan M. Wai, *The African-Arab Conflict in the Sudan* (New York & London: Africana Publishing Co., 1981)

Yosa Wawa, *Southern Sudanese Pursuits of Self-Determination: documents in political history* (Kisubi: Marianum Press, 2005)

Salim Charles Wilson, *I Was a Slave* (London, nd [c.1939])

Peter Woodward, *Condominium and Sudanese Nationalism* (London: Rex Collings, 1979)

www.ingramcontent.com/pod-product-compliance
Lightning Source LLC
Chambersburg PA
CBHW021124300426
44113CB00006B/279